How CEOs
and the Business
Roundtable
Hijacked
the World's
Greatest Wealth
Machine—
And How to
Get It Back

CORP OCRACY

Robert A. G. Monks

BICENTENNIAL
1807
WILEY
2007
BICENTENNIAL

John Wiley & Sons Inc.

Library of Congress Cataloging-in-Publication Data

Monks, Robert A. G., 1933–
    Corpocracy : how CEOs and the business roundtable hijacked the world's greatest wealth machine and how to get it back / Robert A. G. Monks.
        p. cm.
    ISBN 978-0-470-14509-8 (cloth)
    1. Corporations—Moral and ethical aspects. 2. Chief executive officers—Moral and ethical aspects. 3. Corporate governance. I. Title.
    HD2741.M588 2008
    174' .4—dc22

                                                                2007026261

Printed in the United States of America.

10 9 8 7 6 5 4 3 2 1

For Bobby

Contents

Preface

I remember the first time I heard the word *corporation*. I was in my father's study in Clipston Grange, a rambling mansion in Lenox, Massachusetts. It was late afternoon of an autumn Sunday in 1940—the adults had been discussing the war in Europe—and I was handling the various objects on the great desk. I had in hand a silver trophy inscribed with the words "St. Mark's School, Intelligence Prize, 2nd Place," and the years "1914," "1915," and "1916." My mother explained that Pa's school gave a general intelligence test and that he was the first Fourth Former (10th grade) ever to finish as high as second. That year and each succeeding year and at Harvard and at Oxford, Pa's best friend and roommate, Porter Chandler, was always first.

Precocious as ever, I asked, "What does Porter Chandler do?"

"He is a corporation lawyer in New York," Mother answered. And thus at the age of seven, I learned what the smartest man in my little world did.

It was, as they say, a shaping experience. So was the recurrent dream I had, beginning at a very young age. I was climbing a stairway cut right to left into the side of a cliff on the north part of Lenox. I carried an object in my right hand—what it was is beyond knowing, but it was neither a cross nor a sword—and always, I was followed by a stream of people. Many years later, when I took my wife to see the cliff, I was horrified to discover that it did not exist outside my subconscious.

Unchallenged inherited values informed the next 30 years of my life. I understood the rules and tried hard to succeed, and I had the aptitudes that schools reward as well as the work habits and motivation associated with professional success. I was also fortunate to have entered this world during the lowest birth year in recent American history, in fact on the very day Prohibition ended. When coupled with early marriage and fatherhood, my age not only exempted me from military service; it also put me into a sparsely populated class in the job markets. As a result, I have enjoyed relatively easy access to the full range of public and private opportunity for going on 60 years.

When I graduated from high school in June 1950, I went to work as a runner for Paine Webber, Jackson and Curtis—an entry-level post that involved delivering stock certificates to other brokerage houses. We runners comprised three distinct types: college and business school graduates starting at the bottom, retired postal carriers, and "specials" like me—a friend of good customers. Within a week, the Korean War broke out, and all the World War II veterans were reactivated. Thus, I instantly became the only new person at the bottom of the chain. This resulted in a curious amalgam of jobs, which relieved the fundamental boredom of the position. The fact is, there wasn't much to do. During the summer of 1950, the daily volume of shares traded on the New York Stock Exchange never exceeded one million. Today, it rarely goes below one billion.

The corporate world slipped mostly from my view during the years I spent as an undergraduate at Harvard, then reemerged when I was a law student. Corporation law at that time was lyrically described by one literate law school dean as "empty corporation statutes—towering skyscrapers of rusting girders internally welded together and containing nothing but wind." Studying corporation law was like learning a wiring diagram: There was no sense of substance. The professor was bright and impatient, so courageously (or stupidly), I waited until after our final class and asked him simply, "Is this all there is?"

"What do you mean?" he asked, after a merciful pause.

"Corporations are huge agglomerations of power within a democratic society," I managed to get out. "How is their power accommodated to the interests of the citizens?"

He blinked and smiled, then said: "You will enjoy a chapter in a book that I am writing." He was right. I have enjoyed it for the past 50 years.

For the first dozen years after law school, I became an integral part of that agglomeration of power I had so naïvely inquired about. As a corporate lawyer and venture capitalist and through related forays into investment banking and company management, I became familiar with making money and commonsense economics. In general, my training and background served me well in those roles, but a view of life emanating from post-Victorian values had kept me from studying academic economics. Increasingly, the unfamiliar but confident language of university-based economists was creeping into discussions of both business and government policy. To close my learning gap, I took advantage of a six-month hiatus to study macroeconomic theory with a professor who had just returned from a spell on the President's Council of Economic Advisors. My tutor was honest and accessible. I was hungry to absorb the new wisdom—a world in which ultimate virtue was known and could be identified, so different from the religious myths and uncertainties I had grown up with. Everyone talked of economics "laws" and the "science" of economics. I wanted in on the secret.

Later I would conclude that each of these absolutes was demonstrably wrong. There was one law known as the "Phillips Curve," which proved an inverse relationship between the rate of inflation and the unemployment rate—high unemployment meant low inflation; low unemployment had the opposite effect. So popular was this law in the late 1950s that it became the basis for a whole series of policy trade-offs. Yet the Phillips Curve, like many other confident representations that the world's economic function can be understood and managed, posits a condition 180 degrees contrary to the experience of the past 20 years. Sometimes I wonder how these always certain people live with themselves in times of double deficits of unimaginable proportions—deficits all but ignored in the administration of American policy.

Ultimately, what I learned from my study of economics was how little we know. That has helped me avoid being bullied by the clever, but it doesn't relieve a general sense of unease.

As the scene in my father's study suggests, I belonged to a meritocracy of the well-born. It would be churlish to complain of such a luxury, but being gifted with a Midas touch and Midas-like connections can be self-destroying if you have appetites or sensitivities in other directions. The small world of the very wealthy in which I was raised is a homogeneous subculture with rules of behavior as finely tuned as those of Confucius and just as confining. In return for membership in a club based on birth, education, and accomplishment comes a corresponding loss in the ability to understand and to participate in the life of the larger community in which you live. The great homes and remote holiday retreats protect against violence and bother even as they inhibit contact with the people and ideas that form the energizing spirit of society.

That is what I was looking for when I moved to Maine in search of a political career. I had still the little boy's dream of leading, and I could no longer ignore the artificiality of the life my birthright seemed to have set as my destiny. Elective politics turned out to be a pursuit for which I had little talent, but pursuing politics opened my sensibilities to the larger world. I can recall to this day driving past the International Paper Company plants in Livermore Falls early in my never-to-be political career and seeing the Androscoggin River coated with six feet of foam glistening in the sun. Rumor had it, I was told, that if the wind blew the foam on your car, it would destroy the finish.

I immediately understood that *no one* wanted that pollution in the Androscoggin River. I could hear the embarrassed dialogue all around me. Responsible public officials kept saying, "We know that the foam is poisonous, but the community needs the jobs." Company executives would drop their gaze and explain, "We're in a competitive world, and we can't afford expenses that our competitors don't have to pay." The workforce and the townspeople felt themselves caught in a system they could neither understand nor control. Everyone could see the threat the foam posed, but the immutable logic of economics provided no way of dealing with the foam other than simply to endure it and hope it wouldn't blow on your car or your children.

Contemplating that foam introduced me to the unintended consequences of corporate functioning on society and led me to question for the first time whether the great corporation was a creature by Frankenstein. Had humans really succeeded in creating a wealth machine that must destroy us? And thus began what has been my lifework: delineating the underlying dynamics of corporate power to devise a system that combines wealth creation with societal interest. The work has been its own reward.

The irony of moving from hugely successful law and business careers in Massachusetts to repeated political failure in Maine is that through providence, or otherwise, I acquired just those characteristics necessary to make me an honest and effective promoter of good corporate governance: top-level business experience as CEO of substantial companies and interested founder or promoter of many smaller ones; chairmanship of what is always referred to as a "venerable trust company"; director of a dozen listed companies and several governmental corporations; top legal experience as partner in a large corporate law firm; political experience through administrative appointments; and enough money and, more important, the capacity to make money to independently support my efforts. Even my failed forays into elective politics served to harden me to the hostility and rejection that always comes with trying to force new ideas and perspectives on the comfortable status quo.

Over the years, as I struggled to sort out the reality of corporate power from the misleading vocabulary and representations that surround and protect it, I came to gather the sense of a presence. Sometimes, I could identify particular organizations and people—I do that in these pages—but most of the time there was only a firmly felt but poorly understood feeling that a coherent and powerful group masterminded the containment of threats to corporate power.

That sounds a bit paranoid, I realize, but my experience has, in truth, produced a bit of paranoia. The various negotiations I had with Sears Roebuck might have been, for me, the clearest manifestation of this mysterious energy force. In 1981, I mounted an almost successful campaign for a seat on the Sears board. The company was reeling; its business plan was a widely acknowledged disaster. Top management and directors needed shaking up if shareholder value was to be retained, and that's what I set out to do. The company for its part was willing to pay me virtually anything to stop bothering them, but initially, it would not make any changes of a substantive nature. When it finally did make the changes, as it had to for survival, the top officers refused to give me any public credit for having positively influenced their changes even though a famous full-page ad in the *Wall Street Journal* touted a retrenchment I had been urging on the company all along. Why such reluctance? Because I was encountering a system of power, and those who controlled it liked things just the way they were.

The Sears experience educated me more than it angered me. I have been on a lifelong learning quest, and this was a privileged glimpse behind the curtain of the Imperial Corporation. Sometimes, though, I couldn't help becoming enraged. There was the time Jay Lorsch, the hardly revolutionary Harvard Business School professor, was unveiling a book he had coauthored on directors to a small group of interested commentators. The event was sponsored by and held at the book's publisher, the highly respected Harvard Business School Press. Bruce Atwater, then head of General Mills and the Business Roundtable's Corporate Governance Committee, capped a day's bullying with something to this effect: "Institutions like this one had better think twice in publishing this kind of material if they want our continued support." This actually happened. I remember raising my voice in protest. This was the reality of the energy that entrenched the status quo.

There have been other realities to confront: the reality that corporate power has become dominant in the United States and CEO power has become dominant in corporations; the reality that the institutional investors, comprising a majority of ownership of public companies, have turned their backs on their fiduciary duties and acted to entrench the existing system of power; the reality that there has been virtually no enforcement at any level of the obligation of these trustees to consider the primacy, indeed the exclusivity, of their beneficiaries' interests.

Fighting back against such realities has consumed much of the past three-plus decades of my life. Through good fortune, I was appointed in 1983 to head the Department of Labor's division in charge of ERISA, the Employee Retirement Income Security Act of 1974, and from that "bully pulpit" to promulgate the fiduciary requirements of the statute with respect to voting the securities of portfolio companies in the interest of the plan participants. The post was a study in frustration in many ways—the power of entrenched indifference was almost as great as that of the entrenched status quo—but this was an education no graduate school could ever offer.

Because trustees couldn't be expected to inform themselves about the ownership issues for the thousands of companies in their portfolios, I helped launch Institutional Shareholder Services (ISS) to provide cost-effective information and voting services. ISS was an enterprise reacting to proposals from others, so we began LENS to be sure that the most important ownership issues were raised by somebody and that a record would exist showing that activism by owners was value creating. Without doing that, we could never have overcome the reluctance of institutional trustees based on their assumed duty not to waste beneficiaries' money. Although far too many trustees still run from any sort of activism, our work and the work of the many other activist funds we have been involved in over the past decade, both in the United States and England, have shown conclusively that reforming governance pays serious rewards.

Today, we continue to create new enterprises delivering governance information to a world that is increasingly interested in it. Trucost provides environmental impact information. The Corporate Library, which I started with Nell Minow, my long-time partner in many of these enterprises, provides new metrics for measuring the actual cost of bad corporate practice. Nell and I wanted someone else to build TCL. When no one came forward, we did it ourselves.

More than a quarter century of sometimes frantic-seeming efforts has confirmed my conviction that capitalism and its expression in the form of corporations provide the best chance for humankind to improve its lot on earth. For me, it has been a humbling journey with many false turns and hollow enthusiasms. Yet, ultimately, a kind of clarity with respect to the corporate mission has emerged— maximization of profit within rules emanating from legitimate authority. That is the goal, but to get there, we first need to understand the nature of the corporate beast as a complex adaptive system in a newly globalized framework that tends to dilute the effect of traditional national determinations. An adaptive energy cannot be contained within linear rules; it necessitates countervailing energy. At the end, there is no solution short of commitment to process—a process echoing the most fundamental of the United States' constitutional premises.

The only player in the corporate constellation with motivation, competency, and incentive congruent with that of management is ownership. The unforeseen consequence of well-intended federal programs has been to silence a majority of owners at the same time as the leading remaining shareholders have chosen not to be involved. This vacuum of disabled and shirking ownership has caused many of the cancers that characterize the unacceptable present form of the corporate state—what I call the *corpocracy*.

The great author, teacher, and management consultant Peter Drucker introduced the concept of revolutionary change resulting from what he termed "discontinuities": the buildup of tension between a new underlying reality and the surface of established institutions and customary behavior that still conforms to yesterday's underlying realities. While revolutions tend to be violent and spectacular, Drucker argued, discontinuities develop gradually and quietly and are rarely perceived until they have resulted in a volcanic eruption. That's where I am convinced we are at this moment in history. Out-of-control executive pay, neutered boards and ownership, a general unwillingness to exercise fiduciary responsibility, and the absence of an effective counterforce are all indicators of revolutionary change in traditional governance realities. The situation is a given. The question is what to do about it. That, I hope, is what this book answers.

Robert A. G. Monks
Cape Elizabeth, Maine

Acknowledgments

This is the story of a long journey during which I have been nourished by the support of many partners, among them Barbara Sleasman, John Higgins, Ric Marshall, Rick Bennett, and Peter Butler. Nell Minow and I have together written books, started companies, and shared moments of disappointment. What progress has been made is the result of her involvement. I thank Allen Sykes especially. He and I also coauthored a work that anticipates this one and whose diagnoses and proposed solutions have increasing validity today. Allen generously, promptly, and brilliantly provided corrective analysis to several parts of this book—particularly those having to do with modern economics.

Paul Hodgson gave patient years of excellent analysis to my queries about the compensation of American executives. Without the confidence that I could rely on Paul's utter integrity and professionalism, I could not have drawn the essential conclusions on which the book is based. Only such an obviously fair and scholarly work can compel the changing of conventional wisdom. My friend and lawyer, Peter Murray, has kindly molded my fantasies about litigation into a coherent chapter. Ric Marshall made invaluable suggestions to the mode of presentation, including inspiring Figure 5.1, which, in fact, is the work of Alex Higgins and Paul Hodgson.

Many have read drafts of the book and have furnished generous and insightful comments. I thank especially Jack Bogle, David Bollier, Adrian Cadbury, Rich Ferlauto, Alastair Ross Goobey, Paula Gordon, Neva Goodwin, Marc Gunther, Hazel Henderson, George Herrick, Arthur Levitt, Charles Munger, Donald Munro, Ralph Nader, Jesse Norman, "Shad" Roe, Howard Sherman, Les Standiford, Bill Sumner, and Alan Towers.

Howard Means, as editor, combines a fine literary sense, vast knowledge of the subject, and the rare combination of courage and courtesy so welcome to an author. He would not accept less than my best but was most patient in helping me find the way. With the help of his son Nathan, which literally made possible his involvement in this project, Howard was able to reduce the content of the book by half and to improve its quality by an equivalent amount. Being involved with Howard in writing a book makes a pleasure out of a process otherwise trying.

From John Wiley & Sons, Inc. one could ask no more. Larry Alexander believed in the book and wouldn't give up, when most would; Emily Conway was prompt, kind, and helpful.

Notwithstanding so much help and advice, the entire responsibility for the contents rests with me.

Cor·poc·ra·cy [fr. L *corpus* body + Gk-*kratia* power, rule] government by the corporation; that form of government in which the sovereign power resides in corporations, and is exercised either directly by them or by elected and appointed officials acting on their behalf.

Chapter One

AN AUDIENCE WITH THE EMPEROR

May 28, 2003

The temperature was already bordering on hot as I approached the Morton H. Meyerson Symphony Center a little before nine in the morning. Located north of downtown Dallas, the Meyerson is reached via a miniplaza adorned with sculptures and plantings. Over the past 14 years, the venue has housed countless musical performances, banquets, rehearsals, even film shoots. Today's audience was there for a different kind of entertainment: corporate theater—ExxonMobil's Annual Meeting.

The day before, eight protestors from the Greenpeace environmental movement had run around outside Exxon's Irving, Texas, headquarters in tiger suits, an ironic tribute to the company's famous spokesanimal. More protestors must have been expected this morning because the Meyerson entrance was protected by barriers and sawhorses and watched over by police. In fact, only a few dozen demonstrators had turned up, pluckily acting out the philosopher's classic conundrum: If a tree falls in the forest and no one hears it, is there any sound?

Shareholders were also few and far between, maybe 200 of us in all, an infinitesimal fraction of the hundreds of thousands of people around the globe who own a stake in the company individually or through one or more mutual funds. It wasn't that ExxonMobil was unimportant—far from it. As I write, it's the largest corporation in the history of the planet judged by market value—something on the order of half a trillion dollars, larger than the national budget of France.

Nor was there any absence of issues to discuss. Exxon has been blamed for everything from despoiling the environment to harassing gay employees and backing foreign governments in their efforts to drive rebels out of potentially oil-rich provinces. The Greenpeace demonstrators of the day before were only the surface manifestation of a widely held belief that Exxon is one of the world's worst corporate citizens, and Exxon didn't seem to mind in the least.

Then-CEO Lawrence Rawl's 1989 explanation that he was "too busy" to visit the *Exxon Valdez* oil tanker while it was gushing 30 million gallons of crude into Alaska's Prince William Sound might have been the most headline-grabbing gaffe, but current CEO Lee Raymond had done his best to stoke the fires. Raymond's outspoken resistance to the science of global warming, to the Kyoto Accords, and to fossil-fuel alternatives had spurred concern not just from hard-core environmentalists but from an order of nuns in New Jersey and shareholder groups inside Exxon. Raymond's stances had even isolated his company from the other colossi of the oil world, many of which had begun promoting the possibilities of renewable fuels. Under Lord John Browne's leadership, BP was already claiming that its initials stood not just for British Petroleum but for "Beyond Petroleum."

There were intracompany issues as well. No one was faulting Raymond for his financial stewardship of Exxon. The gross operating profit in 2002 had been a healthy $35 billion. 2003 promised to be even better, and the future looked limitless. By December 2005, the *Economist* magazine would declare, "Raymond could claim to be the most successful oil boss since Rockefeller." The question was, in a publicly held company, did he deserve compensation that even the rapacious John D. Rockefeller might have admired?

In 2003, according to *Forbes*, Raymond would be paid $23 million, an income near the top of Fortune 500 executives. To be sure, even such an astronomical figure was generally in step with the explosion in executive compensation through the 1980s and 1990s. While many stocks and shareholders did quite well over that same period, the growth in executive earnings far outstripped the growth of the S&P 500—by a ratio of roughly 2:1.

Arguably, too, Raymond and his peers were even underpaid by comparison with leading entertainers and professional athletes. Eighteen miles down Tom Landry Highway in Arlington, shortstop Alex Rodriguez and his Texas Rangers would lose 6 to 4 to the Tampa Bay Devil Rays on the night of Exxon's annual meeting, on the way to a disappointing 91-loss season. Nonetheless, A-Rod, as he is known, would be rewarded that fall by the New York Yankees with a 10-year $252-million contract, slightly more on an annualized basis than Lee Raymond's 2003 pay. Raymond at least had a record operating profit to show for his troubles.

Still, if the owners of Exxon's 6.7-billion outstanding shares had been able to vote on his $23-million salary, quite a few might have been willing to turn the company over to some capable person willing to take a mere $5 or $10 million for the privilege of running the company. That was one in-house issue that needed airing, or so many of us felt. The other was one of my ongoing battles with the company: whether to require that the positions of chairman and CEO be filled by two different people. At present, Raymond held both posts, a situation akin to having the president of the United States serve simultaneously as chief justice of the Supreme Court. Alex

Rodriguez might have made slightly more money than Lee Raymond in 2003, but he couldn't approve his own raises or his own perks on top of the raises. In effect, Raymond could do just that.

One might reasonably ask why, with so much potentially on the table, so few ExxonMobil owners had bothered to attend? Annual meetings are the one time each year when management is legally required to make itself accessible to shareholders, the only time we owners can put questions to those who oversee our money. No one expects CEOs and corporate directors to rise to the level of Periclean Athens, but in theory annual meetings should be a time for taking the long view of the enterprise, for raising and answering— via shareholder resolutions and floor questions—vital concerns about its place in society and its broader mission, even for parsing the books with an outsider's eye. In practice, of course, annual meetings are anything but.

Over the past seven decades, corporate lawyers, with the complicity of the Securities and Exchange Commission (SEC), have waged a relentless war against a "shareholder democracy." Today, any meaningful participation by shareholders at an annual meeting can be easily quashed, while any shareholder resolution that the SEC actually does require a company to include on its proxy statement is virtually certain to have no real significance. My own history with Exxon is a case in point.

In 2002, Exxon was allowed by the SEC to exclude my resolution to separate the CEO and chairman positions even though its required *inclusion* was common practice. Instead, the company's artful and highly compensated legal counsel managed to persuade the commission that my resolution was really a disguised solicitation for votes to replace Lee Raymond on the board and therefore excludable under existing SEC rules. Given that there were only as many nominees on the proxy card as there were vacancies, the argument was absurd on its face, but such absurdities have nourished the corporate bar for many decades.

In 2004, there was no challenge by the company to this same resolution, and it was approved by better than one in four Exxon shareholders who submitted proxy votes prior to the annual meeting. The next year was an atrocity: The same word-for-word, comma-for-comma resolution was rejected in 2005 by the SEC on the grounds that it would be "impossible" for the company to comply with. As with monarchies and oligarchies, so with the SEC; there is no appeal from censorship, no matter how arbitrary.

The SEC was one disincentive to attend. ExxonMobil's caustic chairman/CEO was another. Raymond not only acts the emperor; he actually seems to enjoy it. At this same meeting two years prior, he had belittled shareholders who opposed his positions, while allowing another shareholder with whom he agreed to digress at length. That drew a protest from Shelley Alpern, a shareholder sponsoring a resolution to ban employee discrimination based on sexual orientation.

"I thought our comments were supposed to be linked to the proposal," Alpern said, according to the *Wall Street Journal.*

"True," Raymond sarcastically responded, "I assure you if *you* tried to do that, I would enforce the rules."

Good to his word, Raymond intervened later in the same meeting during the passionate plea of activist Radhi Darmansyah to halt the violence in Banda Aceh. (Exxon has been accused of colluding with the brutal military government of Indonesia.)

"They are murdering my brothers and sisters," Darmansyah lamented in halting English.

Murder or not, at exactly two minutes, the officially allotted time, Raymond stopped Darmansyah, suggesting he could "come back another time." With that, Darmansyah's microphone went dead, and security guards moved closer to be sure he returned to his seat.

Were those of us who did attend the 2003 meeting with the intention of braving Raymond's ire the few, the proud, the brave? Were we idealists or borderline delusional? In truth, we were probably something of all three. Shareholder activists inevitably owe a debt to Don Quixote. As we shuffled toward the entrance to the Meyerson, you could almost hear our shabby armor clanking.

At the entrance to the Meyerson, I presented my ticket and began negotiating security. Previously, I had transferred all my written materials about Exxon into a single file folder, another house rule, and cleared my leather wallet of any of the miscellany I usually carry with me. The clean wallet got me through the metal detector, but afterward, I had to hand my papers over to a woman clearly in distress over how to do her job. She twice called over her supervisor, who eventually told her, "It's a matter of your judgment." No question, he'll go far in Exxon.

In fact, I had the feeling that both the paper checker and her boss knew exactly who I was and were passing the word on. Was this just my old paranoia or was it the result of all the attention? Indeed, might not paranoia be the purpose of all the attention? Shareholders who have already experienced the baseless guilt brought on by even the routine questioning of security agents are surely more likely to be self-censoring and politely deferential when they finally get their chance to speak.

The anterooms at the Meyerson worked well for the small number of attendees. Strolling around the open spaces, I listened to the company's explanation of its policies on upstream logistical problems and global warming. Later, I made myself known to a man identified by his badge as a corporate official, asking him whether I could be introduced to any of the directors of the corporation who I presumed were available. He assured me that they were but that he personally did not know a director and therefore couldn't help. I remember thinking that ignorance must be bliss.

The arrangement of acoustic baffles allows for two doors through which to enter the concert hall, and the two doors, in turn, allowed for yet another level of security. Inside, though, the Meyerson was almost cozy. We had been told that there would be two microphones—one for proponents of the resolutions and the other for opponents. As the mover of Resolution 9, I asked the attendant whether the blue-scarved seats were reserved for proponents. They were, which enabled me to accommodate my overlength legs in the aisle.

All the board members were positioned in slightly raised seats to the left of the stage, which was guarded by pairs of armed police officers. This was a meeting by the rules. Ten minutes could be spent on each of the nine shareholder resolutions. The mover was allowed four minutes, which could be split between opening statement and rebuttal. Each person subsequently desiring to talk had two minutes. A mover and three commentators were permitted. Green, yellow, and red lights on each microphone and on each side of the stage let speakers know when they were reaching the end of the line. When the light turned red, an increasing level of auditory static was projected—doubtless as a courtesy to the impaired. As usual, more people wanted to speak than had been allotted time slots, but we all knew the rules and that they would be scrupulously enforced.

A very attractive blue backdrop had been projected with ''ExxonMobil, 121st Annual Meeting'' and three views of Earth from space. At the sides stood two flags—American on the left and Texan on the right. Framed by this galactic setting, CEO and Chairman Lee Raymond entered the stage from the right precisely at 9:00 a.m. and convened the meeting.

Raymond had joined Exxon in 1963 as a chemical engineer, before moving into management roles in the 1970s. In 1984, he was named a senior vice president and elected to the board, becoming president in 1987. Raymond took over as chairman and chief executive officer (CEO) of Exxon in 1993. Six years later, he engineered the $82-billion takeover of Mobil, creating the world's biggest publicly traded oil company.

Raymond launched the meeting with a well-produced, genuinely powerful account of the state of the company. ExxonMobil is something new in the history of the world—a sophisticated enterprise bristling with new technology and operating in more than 200 countries or territories, from Equatorial Guinea to Venezuela to the Russian Far East. The British Empire at the height of its power had less reach and far less capacity to generate profit. I had more than a passing interest in the profit side of the equation. Ram Trust Services, which is my family office, then managed in excess of 100,000 shares of ExxonMobil, which on the day of the 2003 annual meeting would close at $36.45 a share, a figure that would double over the next three-and-a-half years.

Once Raymond had finished his report, we moved on to the first item of business—the election of directors. This was a unique possibility for real discussion as the 10-minute overall time limit was not imposed. Anybody who had managed to find a way into the concert hall could get in his or her two minutes' worth.

The charismatic Franciscan Michael Crosby started with a point of order and ended wrangling with Raymond, who rather disappointingly retreated to New Jersey law and "I make the rules here." Then Public Issues Committee Chair Phil Lippincott was targeted for abuse. He was asked to explain what had been done during the year on the subject of global warming. Lippincott had no microphone and no obvious enthusiasm to answer the question, but Lee Raymond answered for him by saying this was a board issue and the board had considered the question appropriately. End of discussion. Finally, about an hour and twenty minutes after convening—precisely at 10:20, no fooling around here—we turned to confirming the auditors and approval of the 2003 executive incentive program, all of which went unsurprisingly smoothly.

With that, we moved on to the nine shareholder resolutions that had somehow found their way past the SEC censors. When we finally came to Number 9, my resolution to separate the CEO and chairman positions, I stood up and approached the microphone.

"As we speak," I began, "the great nations are meeting in St. Petersburg for the G-7 summit. It is not beyond possibility that sometime in the future they will expand their number. If they did so, ExxonMobil could be invited to the meeting, as it is today the 21st largest economic system in the world. And, Mr. Chairman, you have less restraints on the exercise of power than any of the leaders of countries today. You are effectively less accountable than the assembled presidents, prime ministers, or chancellors. The scope of your operations is global, and goes beyond the usual language of business into politics and foreign policy. The scope of your power, Mr. Chairman, is truly imperial. You are an Emperor."

As I moved to sit down, Raymond demurred, but he didn't exactly look upset at his imperial prospects. Then the proponents and opponents of my resolution debated until Raymond, constantly aware of the clock, called me up again. My opening statement had taken exactly one minute and 23 seconds. For my closer, the always exact Raymond reminded me, "You have two minutes and thirty-seven seconds."

This time, I turned to talk directly to the directors.

"In referring to you as Emperor, Mr. Raymond, I meant no disrespect. I use this language to point out the real nature of the problem of governance for ExxonMobil. You have the nature of a country. The board must think more in terms of the mode developed for a national system and stop trying to apply the business precedents that Exxon-Mobil has grown beyond. As Americans, we must think with pride of the care that the Framers of our Constitution organized a system in which the power of the Chief Executive was effectively accountable to that of a Congress and a Supreme Court. ExxonMobil is an empire, and the board needs to look at the political model to find a counterforce for the power of the executive. Mr. Raymond, if you don't like what I say, you have only yourself to blame. You are a victim of your own success, and, remember—Napoleon Bonaparte had his Talleyrand."

The yellow light was on as I finished. I remember feeling a surge of victory that I had crammed everything I wanted to say into such a thin time frame. Then I realized, "Oh, my God, they have me thinking like them."

The clock tolled the end of the meeting as Sister Pat Daly implored the chairman to take note of the mockery over which he was presiding—the needless restrictions on share-holder communication, the minatory security apparatus, the anal fixation on the clock, the obvious enlistment of "bought" testimony on particular resolutions.

Afterward, I walked out of Meyerson into the noonday Dallas spring with chapters of Russian history flashing through my mind. Maybe it was my talk of emperors. A hundred years ago, the masses respectfully petitioned the Tsar for reform. But the enduring image was the Show Trials of the 1930s. We were all playing roles, reciting the lines allocated to us by our masters. I felt diminished—no, I felt dirty—for having participated in this charade.

Give Exxon credit: It has no problem producing the same stale theater year after year. At the same meeting held in the same location on May 26, 2004, the treasurer of the state of Maine, Dale McCormick, representing the Maine State Retirement System, moved to ask a question. The exchange is worth reporting in full, from Exxon's own videotape of the meeting:

> McCormick: Good Morning, Mr. Raymond, I'm Dale McCormick, the Treasurer of the great State of Maine. (*applause*) Ah, I see people have been to our fair State and come again, please. I'm an Institutional Investor. I represent many Institutional Investors, and I'd like to know if the auditor is here so that I might pose a question?
>
> Raymond: Mr. Patterson, right down here.
>
> McCormick: Great, hello Mr. Patterson. I'd like to know what provisions you have made on the financial statements for damage caused by climate change. Climate change is a potential liability and I wonder if you have reserved for it on the balance sheet?
>
> Patterson: The responsibility for provisions in the financial statements are those of management, and I'm not sure that I am the appropriate person to respond to that question.
>
> McCormick: Thank you. Then may I pose that question to Mr. Houghton, who is the chair of the audit committee?
>
> Raymond: You may not.
>
> McCormick: Why, sir?
>
> Raymond: Because that's not — the audit committee looks at the recommendations of management.

That's properly the responsibility of the controller of the corporation.

McCormick: May I pose it to you?

Raymond: Oh, sure. You can pose anything to me. (*laughter*)

McCormick: Will you answer me?

Raymond: Oh, that's a different question? (*more laughter*)

McCormick: Sir, I do not think it is a matter of laughter when an institutional investor representing over 3 million shares cannot get answers to an important question like this.

Raymond: The question is precisely what?

McCormick: What provisions have you made on the financial statements for the damage caused by climate change and the potential liability there?

Raymond: It's neither likely nor could it be estimated.

End of scene, but not end of story. The emperor decides who will be allowed to ask questions and who will be allowed to answer them. That in this instance he could feel free to trivialize a question that compels the attention of most of the people on Earth is the clearest possible indication of the state of corporate power within the United States at the present time.

Two years later, I resumed my role in the charade with the same resolution I had advanced in 2003. This time, I changed tack slightly and wrote some weeks before the annual meeting to the entire board. In the letter, I acknowledged Exxon's superlative operating record. "The important question for the board now," I wrote, "is to devise an appropriate strategy to make the most profitable company in the history of business the best company in the world for the foreseeable future."

Among the issues to be considered, again to quote myself:

Why is our company the one with the bull's eye on its chest? Why are we the target of so much hostility? Is this simply envy of our size and profitability? Is there a particular confrontational Exxon style that is essential to our quality of operation? Do we have to be ornery to be successful? Or are we needlessly creating antagonism in a world that does not always accommodate the efficient operation of large companies?

All those issues, I wrote, are important, as are the perceptions that Exxon has inappropriate influence over government, especially on environmental matters: that it earns too much money and does little with the excess profit it does earn other than to sit on it; and that it is indifferent to its obligations to be a good corporate citizen.

"In sum," I ended, "there is basis to conclude that Exxon 'dances to a different drummer' and in doing so invites all constituencies to interpret its activities from an unfavorable perspective. Even though we are the biggest company in the world, does it make sense—almost as bravado—to defy human needs to be able to relate to us?"

I asked at the meeting whether anybody had read my letter, but there was no response. When I requested from the chairman extra time to read it to them, the audience lent me substantial support, but from the chair I met only inflexibility. I have abbreviated the preceding content both because I believe the questions I raised in this letter are the kind corporations should answer to someone and because I know from years of experience that no one in the United States today can elicit any such responses as a matter of right or law.

I wasn't alone in writing Exxon's top management. In October 2006, five months after I had sent my letter, U.S. senators Olympia Snowe, a Maine Republican, and John D. Rockefeller IV, the West Virginia Democrat, wrote to the chief executive officer and board of directors of ExxonMobil:

We are writing . . . as U.S. Senators concerned about the credibility of the United States in the international community, and as Americans concerned that one of our most prestigious corporations has done much in the past to adversely affect that credibility. We are convinced that ExxonMobil's longstanding support of a small cadre of global climate change skeptics, and these skeptics' access to and influence on government policymakers, have made it increasingly difficult for the United States to demonstrate the moral clarity it needs across all facets of its diplomacy. Obviously, other factors complicate our foreign policy. However, we are persuaded that the climate change denial strategy carried out by and for Exxon-Mobil has helped foster the perception that the United States is insensitive to a matter of great urgency for all of mankind, and has thus damaged the stature of our nation internationally.

Maybe a letter from such high councils ultimately will have an effect. Maybe the fact that the letter is cosigned by the great grandson and namesake of the founder of Standard Oil, Exxon's progenitor, will carry the day in the long run. But the signs are not hopeful.

Lee Raymond had been gone for nearly two years by the time the letter was sent, escorted serenely into his golden years with a retirement package worth an estimated $400 million, awarded by the grateful board of directors he had so long chaired. In his place, ExxonMobil was now being run by Rex Tillerson. Like his predecessor, Tillerson assumed the dual titles of CEO and chairman. After all, why should an emperor be accountable to anyone but himself?

Chapter Two

ECONOMICS ASCENDANT

The author James Baldwin once wrote with great insight, "The root function of language is to control the universe by describing it." As Baldwin suggests, language gives us a way of tackling and containing the great mysteries of existence. It is the foundation of religion, of philosophy, of our systems of government. But language also migrates. Words change meaning, or new meanings are forced on them or wrung out of them. The genius of George Orwell's *1984* doesn't lie in imagining the ultimate totalitarian state—Orwell had a ready example of that in front of him. The true genius lies in the way Oceana's totalitarians manipulate language to create an alternate reality. In Orwell's New-Speak, "war" becomes "peace," "love" is "hate," "Big Brother" rules with a smothering iron hand.

As with governments, so with corporations. We understand them through the language we use to describe them, yet the words constantly struggle with one another to increase their power and prestige, much like the ferocious competition between brands. Take the phrase *maximizing wealth.* For generations, it was understood that publicly held corporations would promote a politically defined objective of the general good and that their managers would strictly limit the application of power to optimize the interest of the beneficial owners: the shareholders. This was, in essence, the social contract that freed corporations to maximize wealth.

Today, at least in the United States, that understanding no longer holds. Maximizing wealth has shed its obligations to the general good. Almost everyone now understands wealth maximization to be an unquestionable good in its own right— a worthy explanation of a corporation's objectives and goals even if that means quashing other concerns about corporate citizenship such as pollution, deceptive accounting, or tax evasion. Good deeds are for Eagle Scouts. Big Business's goodness is measured in profit and loss.

As they were with so many things not related to production and sales, CEOs and other corporate interests were initially slow to catch on to the importance of these word-struggles. The bottom line was what mattered, not the linguistic envelope that Big Business operated within. That, too, has changed dramatically. Over the past three decades, corporations have been employing well-funded armies of top legal talent and alleged experts not just to win court battles and favorable legislation but to change the very language that we use to describe their activities and, in the process, to alter our understanding of the basic nature of corporate responsibility.

The rapid spread of this new corporate language has been helped along by many events—the rise of global competition, an almost unbroken string of largely pro-business presidential administrations, even an entire branch of the media devoted to business, corporate news, and commentary. But no single factor has been more important than the ascendancy of a once-overlooked and devalued discipline: economics.

Like corporations, economics today enjoys a much more privileged standing in the world than it once did. Often mocked as the "dismal science"—after Thomas Carlyle's famous phrase—economics began to emerge as its own discipline separate from philosophy with the 1776 publication of Adam Smith's landmark *Wealth of Nations*. But even

Adam Smith could carry the ball only so far. As a social science that attempted to quantify the human exchange of resources, economics faced constant scorn from other academic fields, particularly the so-called hard sciences, for not being sufficiently scientific.

This distaste for economics was never clearer than in 1969 when the first Nobel Prize in Economics was awarded. Created on the initiative of the Bank of Sweden and not by Alfred Nobel's will as was the case with, say, physics or literature, the new prize immediately faced charges of being an imposter award. Peter Nobel, a descendant of Alfred, has carried the fight forward to the present day, claiming the prize amounts to trademark infringement of the family name. "There is no mention in the letters of Alfred Nobel that he would appreciate a prize for economics," Peter Nobel told one interviewer. "The Swedish Riksbank, like a cuckoo, has placed its egg in another very decent bird's nest."

Other objections—many originating in the university, but widely repeated in the mainstream press—raised the old charge that economics was not science proper and that the discipline failed to contribute sufficiently to human advancement to merit the prestige of a Nobel Prize. This argument even carried some weight with economists themselves, including the 1974 Nobel winner, Gunnar Myrdal, who later admitted publicly to his discipline's shortcomings.

Nonetheless in December 1969, in the Grand Auditorium of the Concert Hall in the center of Stockholm, Norwegian Ragnar Frisch and the Dutchman Jan Tinbergen bowed to the King of Sweden as the first two recipients of the Bank of Sweden Prize in Economic Sciences in Memory of Alfred Nobel. Since then, and despite the initial outcry, the enormous prestige of the Nobel Prize has done as much as anything to legitimate economics as a science. Every year one or more economists stands on a par with that year's giants of the natural sciences—a moment that opens the door to imagining economics as being as politically neutral as mathematics.

Simultaneously, perhaps because it was easier to determine contest winners by quantifiable measures than by more abstract expressions of genius, modern economics began to gain a sharp ascendancy over the classical version of the discipline. Classical economics had its roots in moral philosophy. Indeed, Adam Smith had trained as a moral philosopher and had once been as well known for the *Theory of Moral Sentiments* as he was for the *Wealth of Nations.* In the classical understanding, an economist was expected to be anchored in history, politics, morality, and sociology as well as in the manipulation and interpretation of numbers. Economists were equally expected to function in and be acute observers of the real world. As the late 19th-century economist Alfred Marshall once put it, "Economics is the study of mankind in the ordinary business of life."

Like modern economists, classical ones assumed that rational people will try to maximize their personal satisfaction, but unlike modern ones, they didn't equate "personal satisfaction" almost exclusively with wealth. To the classicists, it was equally probable that one might seek to maximize leisure or social life or moral behavior—whatever might most improve quality of life, not solely one's assets or income. To classical economists, the term *cost-benefit analysis* is almost an oxymoron. Since the true cost of anything is properly measured not by what is paid for it but by what is forgone to get it—the so-called opportunity cost—and since benefit is subject to unquantifiable subjective judgments, analysis in a numerical sense is all but impossible.

The two schools of economic thought also differ sharply on the limits of corporate responsibility. The ascendant, modernist branch likes to run away from the long-term consequences of such external corporate issues as degradation of water quality; but classic economists have trouble doing that, trained as they are in multiple disciplines and duty-bound to observe the "ordinary business of life." For example, external benefits might justify subsidies for education, while external costs would justify government intervention to curtail pollution. Efficiency is similarly complicated for classicists. Can we judge markets for slaves, prostitution, and weapons of mass destruction solely on whether they are efficient? Of course not, the classicists would say, but for the time being, the classical economists have lost the war within the discipline, routed by the gospel of numbers. When I use the terms *economics* and *economists* in the pages that follow, I am referring to the modernists and modern economics.

Modern economics certainly makes use of all the paraphernalia of the hard sciences: quantification of input, formulas, tabular representation of results, and so on. These characteristics of value-free objectivity and exacting precision create the impression that such a thing as a law or a science of economics actually exists while investing economics with its mystique and predominant role in all sorts of worldwide public policy making, not just fiscal policy. Ever since the first economics Nobel was awarded, there has been a growing tendency to apply economic modes of thought to fields from law to medicine and education.

As the sweep of economics broadens, so does the power of its language. The vocabulary of economics encourages a fixation on precise numerical expression and an almost magical belief in its efficacy, further entrenching economics at the core of decision making and understanding. All this might be okay if life really were a finely tuned machine in every regard, but of course, it's not. Economics focuses us on the precise and quantifiable, while the imprecise and unquantifiable spill out all over the place. Simply denying the existence of subjective activity in the world of human affairs, as economics does for the most part, doesn't eliminate the subjective's existence from the world, but it does blind us to the potency of the immeasurable.

Stock markets, to cite an obvious example, are bathed in measurements: price-earnings ratio, Beta indexes, year-to-date performance, sector comparisons. Yet the cataclysmic events during which fortunes are often made and lost— market bubbles and bursts—are irrational and subjective in the extreme. We overbuy. We undersell. We run with the bulls and flee with the bears despite what logic tells us, precisely because we are human and fallible. Nonetheless, the vocabulary of economics continues to echo through this and other fields, changing the way people from all walks of life approach questions and even personal decisions that seem far beyond the realm of economics.

Not so long ago, the very notion of a cost-benefit analysis was mostly confined to the business schools. Now running such an analysis seems reasonable, even mandatory in almost any decision: choosing a gift, visiting a friend, buying ingredients for a birthday cake, having a second child. To be sure, it makes sense to weigh costs and benefits in situations that are not strictly economic or fiscal in nature, but accepting this phrase and methodology as crucial to a broad range of decision making is to allow that all human activity can be quantified—that all value can be expressed as a number. As cost-benefit analysis spreads its logic outside economics, we no longer consider whether a particular proposal is good or bad, wise or foolish, but simply whether it is cost-effective.

The famous management mantra "We can manage what we can measure" provides another example both of economics' relentless drive toward the quantifiable and of the way corporations manage to hide behind the veil of objectivity. Remember CEO Lee Raymond's decree at ExxonMobil's 2004 Annual

Meeting regarding whether the potential costs of global warming would be included in the budget: "It's neither likely nor could it be estimated." In short, if global warming doesn't appear in my spreadsheet, it doesn't exist.

Although the corporate-speak leaned on by Exxon's CEO and the language of economics are not totally congruent, they run close enough together to feed off each other and create many widely circulated and powerful terms and myths. Among them:

- *Efficiency:* Over the past several decades has any single criterion been more valued than the *efficiency* of material self-interest? Today when we describe some governmental activity in a positive sense, we no longer talk of it as being legitimate, or beneficial or deleterious for the public, but rather as being efficient and businesslike. An additional assumption of this term is that the free-market-based activities are always the most efficient; yet the much-vaunted efficiency of corporations is often an illusion because the current framework for determining what is efficient ignores all externalized costs, instead displacing them onto other people and nature.

- *Externalization:* In corporate and economic languages, *externalities* are a myth. On the one hand, economics assumes they don't exist. On the other hand, corporations exert full pressure—political and otherwise—to assure that their burden rests on others. In the case of Exxon, this applies to any costs, often very real and large, that don't end up on the company's balance sheet but are instead picked up by governments, individuals, or other corporations: the cost, say, of pollution or of the contribution of internal-combustion engines to global warming. In fact, externalization is perhaps best described as a clown throwing a pie at another clown who ducks, leaving an innocent bystander with a pie-covered face. (The clown scene, by the way, appears in the documentary film *The Corporation* while Milton Friedman, the 1976 Nobel Laureate in Economics, and I are waxing far less eloquently on the same subject.) Corporations and many others pretend the pie doesn't exist precisely because the languages of corporations and economics encourage a silo worldview in which each entity and transaction is examined within its own framework, and the impact each has outside this framework is ignored.

- *GAAP:* The very acronym GAAP (for Generally Accepted Accounting Principles) conjures up spreadsheets, pasty-skinned number crunchers in green eyeshades, and rigorous methodology. In fact, a more accurate acronym these days might be *GWAP*, as in "Gee, Whatever, Accounting Principles." It was under GAAP's watch that Enron imploded, done in by human greed and by accounting practices and principles that bore a striking resemblance to situation ethics. Four years later and despite supposed legislative remedies, GAAP increasingly denotes a mere legal codification of corporate language, rather than any meaningful system of checks and balances.

By widely dispersing a corporate language of terms and phrases such as these, business has gained an upper hand before the opening whistle is even blown. Once the primacy of efficiency is accepted, once a cost-benefit analysis seems not just wise but mandatory and GAAP provides blocking to hide behind, corporations can claim both a home-field advantage and a sympathetic crew of officials in any contest—regulatory, legal, or otherwise. This advantage not only enjoys a global spread; it permeates through many different disciplines and fields of inquiry. As David Leonhardt wrote in the January 10, 2007 *New York Times*, "Economists have been acting a lot like intellectual imperialists in the last decade or so. They have been using their tools—mainly the analysis of enormous piles of data to tease out cause and effect—to examine everything from politics to French wine vintages."

Often this new dominion of economics is spread with the best of intentions—Leonhardt's article was about an economics PhD student taking on the problem of AIDS in Africa—but whatever the impetus, the effect is the same. Once the economists have softened up the target, corporate language is likely to find a more receptive audience, and corporations can then move in for the kill.

That's part of the story. The other part is that as new languages are introduced, older ones are pushed out, or they mutate to serve new purposes. That, too, has happened with Big Business. Much of the traditional language and structure defining the relationship of corporations to society no longer has the meaning that it had in earlier times. This is apparent in many fields but especially in the newly created discipline of law and economics. The fact that such an academic degree even exists speaks volumes about the increased weight of economics, but what's truly alarming is the clout of some of the discipline's loudest voices and the extent to which they are willing to go to allow economic considerations to undermine age-old understandings of right and wrong.

Douglas Ginsburg, a leading proponent, has essentially held in his writings and rulings that knowingly breaking the law is acceptable so long as the consequences are accepted. And Ginsburg is no lightweight. Not only is he Chief Judge of the U.S. Court of Appeals for the District of Columbia; he's also Distinguished Adjunct Professor of Law at George Mason University, whose Law and Economics Center has received nearly $200,000 in grants from ExxonMobil since 1998, and in alternate years a visiting lecturer at his alma mater, the University of Chicago Law School. He might have been a Supreme Court justice as well if his 1987 nomination to the court hadn't been derailed when he admitted to occasional marijuana use in former days.

Ginsburg's thinking—most frequently applied to regulatory law—fits nicely into a spreadsheet-oriented model of the world. In this universe, a responsible corporation that violates an environmental regulation would be expected to account for possible sanctions in their budget but not to recognize they were willfully defiling part of the planet or breaking the law of the land in which they operate. So much for the idea that, in a free society, laws are the legitimate expression of public will and compliance is the ultimate responsibility of citizenship, an obligation that easily transcends mere considerations of cost. In Ginsburg's bad-man view of the legal terrain, people and corporations are motivated not by moral or social obligation but by the simple desire (or nondesire, depending on cost-benefit analysis) to avoid sanctions.

The language of economics also has pervasive significance for those responsible for government administration. When I was the responsible officer in the Department of Labor for the administration of the Employees' Retirement Income Security Act of 1974—commonly known as ERISA—I devoted a great deal of thought to the scope of fiduciary responsibility for ownership of these securities. The pension holdings that fell under ERISA's purview were the largest single component of public ownership of common stock, about 20 percent of the total. As the largest shareholder in public companies, should pension funds be required to act as a human being would act with respect to their rights and responsibilities as owner of public companies? I put the question to Jay Forrester, one of the great business theorists of our time. I can recall his answer still, almost word for word.

Forrester replied crisply and simply that he was opposed to the notion because it would tend to impede the workings of the marketplace. "Pension funds add to the complexity of the economic system," he said. "They reduce an individual's feeling of participation, add to the costs and inefficiency of increased overhead, move the structure of the economy in the direction of bureaucratic socialism, and represent trends opposite to the public quest for smaller and more understandable social structures."

The message was clear: The exercise of responsible ownership amounted to little more than friction and inefficiency in Forrester's calculation. The notion of fiduciary obligations simply does not compute in the world of economics. The decision-making dominance of economics trumps social duty just as the language of economics trumps and subverts the language of moral philosophy.

In the debate about globalization, the language of economics has even obliterated traditional political alignments and long-standing political horse sense. The Democratic Party, which historically fought to protect domestic labor interests and which counted on Big Labor for its votes, has in the past decade or so accepted the logic of maximum wealth creation through encouraging a global system. With the Democrats' compliance, Congress has on several occasions awarded huge contracts to foreign companies, including contracts for defense-related work, on no other grounds than that doing so would be "economical." Forget about the historic political mandate to preserve jobs and technology for defense manufacture at home—what matters now is cost-effectiveness. The logic of corporate and economic languages means that these otherwise agonizing, if not politically suicidal policy decisions can be justified by a cost-benefit analysis.

The logic of corporate language has also intervened in what was for generations the key element in medical care in the United States: the personal relationship between doctor and patient. Amid well-meaning efforts to provide the highest quality care to the largest possible portion of the population, corporate influence has turned health care into just another product. Patients are customers. Doctors are often interchangeable, part of huge practices formed to benefit from "economies of scale." Too often, what's most prominent about a doctor-patient connection is the fiscal relationship, not the emotional one. Our health care providers know all our statistical measures, but they know less and less about us.

This bottom-line driven approach to medicine has far-reaching impacts. No longer is medical research to be pursued for its own sake—reducing suffering and enhancing the quality of life. Instead, policy experts urge us to consider issues of economic competition above all other considerations in funding research. These comments on stem cell research from David Gergen, an advisor to all recent presidents, are typical: "There is a larger issue in which stem cell research finds itself that also will have some compelling political impact and make a difference politically over time," Gergen told an audience at Harvard's John F. Kennedy School of Government, "and that is the degree to which we find ourselves increasingly, as a nation, in competition with a rising China and a rising India and other nations, which are becoming direct threats to American jobs." All that is true, but shouldn't the argument be made from higher ground than protecting jobs?

In higher education, the economic regimentation of all aspects of the university has become so advanced and pervasive that it has resulted in faculty backlashes, including the 2006 forced retirement of Lawrence Summers as president of Harvard University. Summers is virtually the Crown Prince of Economics—both his mother's and his father's brothers won the Nobel Prize in Economics and he himself won the

Clark Medal as the best economist under the age of 40. As if that wasn't enough, he served as Bill Clinton's last Secretary of the Treasury. One would think that such an impressive resume would have served Summers well in his new role at Harvard, but in fact the habits engrained over a professional lifetime seem only to have shortened his tenure. As the *Economist* reported, Summers "measured all academic life by the standards of economics and mathematics." Fed up with economic-speak and irked by Summers' brusque manner, Harvard faculty members rebelled rather than face departmental budget cuts based on a cost-benefit analysis of the curriculum.

As profound as the impact of an economic mindset has been on the practice of law and medicine, those have been in a sense unintended consequences. The greatest consequence of the triumph of a corporate vocabulary has been the one objective Big Business had in mind from the beginning: untethering the corporation from its traditional restraints and responsibilities.

The United States has long provided one of Earth's most pro-business operating environments; commercial energy is generally allowed full scope to blossom and grow. Businesses, however, were not always unchecked heavyweights. They had obligations to society, to the public good, to the rule of law. By redefining the language by which we talk about corporations, Big Business has largely redefined its own duties: *maximizing wealth, efficiency, externalization.* They are not only all the proof corporations need to justify their own existence; they are a kind of 007 license to operate outside the bounds of the law, whether regulatory or otherwise.

The spread of corporate language and logic has had a similar effect on the fiduciary covenant of trust between a company's directors and its owners or shareholders—

that once-sacred oath made by directors and officers of corporations to always consider first the interests of shareholders.

Not so long ago, fiduciary bonds were considered enduring and unbreakable. As Justice Benjamin Cardozo wrote in *Meinhard v. Solomon,* "Many forms of conduct permissible in a workday world for those acting at arm's length are forbidden to those bound by fiduciary ties. A trustee is held to something stricter than the morals of the marketplace. Not honesty alone, but the punctilio of an honor the most sensitive is then the standard of behavior. As to this there has developed a tradition that is unbending and inveterate."

What a distance we have traveled between that 1928 decision and today. One wonders if Cardozo could even begin to wrap his mind around the argument of Douglas Ginsburg and other law-and-economics proponents that individuals can freely decide whether to follow laws. The fallout, though, is everywhere—and nowhere more visible or damaging to corporate governance than in the redefinition of the fiduciary's role. When trustees are free to treat their fiduciary responsibilities as a business decision, weighing possible liability against compliance costs, then "the morals of the marketplace," to borrow Cardozo's phrase, are triumphant, and the traditional "unbending and inveterate" insistence that a fiduciary is responsible solely to the beneficiary and not to any other interests, including his or her own, is dead and gone.

So thoroughly have old understandings of fiduciary responsibility been trampled that legal dictionaries are starting to get in on that act. The *New Palgrave Dictionary of Economics and the Law* includes this notation from Tamar Frankel: "Some scholars view fiduciary relationships solely as contracts that involve unusually high costs of specification of the parties' terms and monitoring of parties' performance . . . Eliminating fiduciary law as a separate category and its reclassification as contract has far reaching consequences."

Indeed it does. For an example of what happens in such an environment, look at the 2002 merger of Hewlett-Packard (HP) with Compaq. In January 2002, HP retained Deutsche Bank's investment banking division to assist in the hotly contested merger. Although Deutsche Bank was to be paid $1 million guaranteed and another $1 million contingent on the merger being approved, it did not disclose this relationship publicly or internally to other divisions of the company.

On Friday, March 15, 2002, the Deutsche Bank proxy committee cast all 17-million proxies on HP stock it controlled—on behalf of its clients—against the merger. The following Monday, HP management called senior-level officials of Deutsche Bank's investment banking division and asked them to arrange for Hewlett-Packard to make a last-minute presentation to the Deutsche Bank proxy committee. According to a Securities and Exchange Commission (SEC) enforcement decree dated August 19, 2003, the Deutsche Bank investment bankers contacted Deutsche Bank's then-Chief Investment Officer, who agreed to allow HP along with the principal shareholder opposing the merger, to make presentations to the proxy committee the next day.

On the morning of March 19, 2002, immediately following these presentations, the members of the Deutsche Bank proxy committee discussed whether they should switch their vote. During this discussion, the voting members were informed that Deutsche Bank's investment banking division was working for HP on the merger and that HP had an enormous banking relationship with Deutsche Bank. The committee then held a revote. Shortly before shareholder voting on the merger closed, Deutsche Bank personnel succeeded in recasting all 17 million of its clients' votes in favor of the merger.

In this case, the SEC found quite correctly that Deutsche Bank had a material conflict of interest in recasting its clients' proxy votes—score one for the concept of fiduciary responsibility. But not so fast: the SEC's remedy for this blatant wrongdoing was a fine of less than the fees Deutsche Bank had collected. What's more, the merger transaction was allowed to stand.

Even in a case where a branch of the federal government publicly enforced a violation of fiduciary duty, the language of economics emerges victorious. In terms of a cost-benefit analysis, everyone wins: Hewlett-Packard gets its merger, Deutsche Bank gets its fee, and the SEC receives a fine. Everyone wins, except beneficiaries of trusts administered by Deutsche Bank, who saw the bonds of fiduciary conduct trampled. Why? How could it happen? It wasn't that the wrong laws were on the books. The law was clear. The overriding problem is that so many people in key positions have accepted an economic view of the world allowing for willful breaches of law for which fines are extracted. That spells the demise of fiduciary conduct as an operative legal deterrent because it creates an effective reality in which it is entirely permissible to walk away from duty.

The wide-ranging dominance of corporate and economic mindsets in decision making means that even insightful policymakers lack the language necessary to consider alternatives outside our current system. Consider what then-Federal Reserve Chairman Alan Greenspan had to say on the subject of corporate governance during a March 26, 2002, address at the New York University's Stern School of Business: "After considerable soul-searching and many congressional hearings, the current CEO-dominant paradigm, with all its faults, will likely continue to be viewed as the most viable form of corporate governance for today's world. The only credible alternative is for large—primarily institutional—shareholders to exert far more control over corporate affairs than they appear to be willing to exercise."

Greenspan accepts the nonparticipation of fiduciary owners as a fact, not pausing to consider that these institutional owners have legal obligations to behave otherwise. One can't really blame Greenspan for that. Where only the language of economics has informing validity, fiduciary and trustee concepts simply do not register. In the land of economic-speak, policy alternatives are few and far between, and almost no one has the words even to express them. And of course, it wasn't the triumph of language alone that turned the policy tide so heavily in Big Business's favor. The corpocracy needed an inside man to hold the lamp and point the way. That was Lewis Powell.

Chapter Three

THE GODFATHER

The corporation is an odd and ancient beast. Clans, tribes, medieval guilds—they all invoked the principle that a collective body be treated as a single entity. The earliest churches and universities were chartered by the state—or more accurately, crown—and granted legal protections and immunities, many of them forerunners of the protections and immunities that today's business corporations enjoy. North America was, in effect, settled by corporations: the Virginia Company, in Jamestown; the Massachusetts Bay Company, in New England; later, the Hudson Bay Company throughout much of what became Canada.

As with the modern business corporation, those earlier corporate bodies pooled individual wealth to achieve goals that no individual acting alone could have accomplished. The combined capital of their stockholders bought ships, established trading posts, bargained for furs, even paid for long rifles to protect agents in an often-hostile New World. For loaning the corporation their money and for assuming the shared risk of the enterprise—ships might sink at sea, or Indians burn and sack the trading posts—the investors in these early corporations properly expected a fair return on investment, just as contemporary shareholders do and should.

Perhaps the most profound difference between the older notion of a corporation and the current one is this: An educated Englishman of the mid-eighteenth century would have understood that the state had granted the corporation legal protections and immunities in the expectation that—in addition to producing a profit—it would be serving a specific public good. By funding and building trade infrastructure, including slave trade, corporations fostered the mercantile system that helped make England rich beyond measure in the Elizabethan and post-Elizabethan ages. By pushing the frontier back and thus opening the United States west of the Appalachians for settlement, they also increased exponentially the value of England's investment in its overseas colony. In short, when corporations did well—when the risks didn't overwhelm them—*and* did good, it was a win-win situation all the way around.

The earliest corporations chartered by the new American colonies and later new states were likewise balanced between profit and public service—water and fire companies and wharf proprietors that hoped to make money for investors while providing essential services and facilitating vital trade. Corporations, though, have long proven their ability to adapt to changing circumstances and differing cultural norms. Look at the way modern Russia has scaled back the rush to privatization in favor of increased state control, or at how the Chinese are inserting political cadres into their larger corporations. So, too, it was with America. The New World was not the old one, and the corporation did not develop here the same way that it had developed in Europe.

For starters, there was the aftertaste of colonialism. Corporations had done the crown's work and had been the crown's instruments, a poor recommendation after the American Revolution. The European model also concentrated economic power in a way that Thomas Jefferson, Andrew Jackson, and their followers instinctively distrusted. That issue came to a head when Jackson took on the Bank of the

United States, the second such institution to be granted a charter by Congress. Jackson's victory in that battle—he instructed his Treasury secretary to stop depositing funds in the bank—took Congress out of the business of chartering and creating corporations for all but the rarest situations: Amtrak, in modern times, to preserve rail passenger travel, and the U.S. Postal Service in an effort to stop the mail system from hemorrhaging money. Instead, the individual states were left to charter the corporations headquartered within them.

That's one way the American-style corporation is unique in the world: essentially localized control, a prerogative jealously guarded by the states and by local and state bar associations whose members profit handsomely from the arrangement. A second distinction is the breadth of ownership. Only in the United States and the United Kingdom are the owners of the largest public companies diversified to the point that no single group generally has a substantial enough share to control the venture. A venture with one million shareholders ultimately has no real owner.

American corporations are also generally free of competition from their own government. While government depends on corporations to create wealth, jobs, and products for the citizenry, the United States has never had a tradition of government ownership of critical industries. Exceptions such as the Tennessee Valley Authority, the United States Synthetic Fuels Corporation, and Fannie Mae are both unusual and almost uniformly controversial. (I write from deep experience in the case of the Synthetic Fuels Corporation since I was one of its founding directors.) In other countries, the continuing dominion of the civil authority over business is unchallenged, even in the United Kingdom where until a quarter century ago the largest companies were owned by the nation.

The U.S. government did retain authority over corporations to the extent that they engaged in interstate commerce, but that has been a rod seldom raised. Even the great "trust buster" Teddy Roosevelt was more inclined to speak loudly and carry a small stick when it came to the powerful vertical trusts that emerged in iron and steel, oil, meatpacking, railroads, and investment banking in the first half century of the Industrial Revolution. Not only was Roosevelt highly selective about the monopolies he went after; his trust-busting crusades often had unintended consequences. On the day that the U.S. Supreme Court ordered the breakup of Standard Oil—May 15, 1911, after 21 years of legal action and 11 separate trials—John D. Rockefeller's net worth was in the range of $300 million. Two years later, Rockefeller's net worth had tripled, and he had maintained control of all 34 companies carved out of the trust he had been ruthlessly building for four decades. (The beautiful symmetry of Standard Oil's history is that in merging Exxon and Mobil, Lee Raymond was reuniting the New Jersey and New York companies that Roosevelt and others had worked so hard to pry apart.)

A final and critical way that the American corporation has traditionally differed from its counterparts around the globe and perhaps the largest reason U.S. corporations have been historically so unfettered lies in the ethos of American-style capitalism. Chartered by centralized governments and in the service of centralized economies, most corporations around the world are expected to serve government-defined ends. Not so the American corporation. Under the American system, the creation of wealth is the highest good, and the corporation that creates the greatest wealth—and the corporate climate that facilitates that creation—thus serves the greatest public end, or so tradition has long held.

By the late 1960s, though, the old verities were in serious disrepair. The civil rights and antiwar crusades had sparked a leftist upsurge. Businesses that a quarter century earlier had been praised for their capacity to turn out munitions in record time found themselves suddenly labeled as war criminals, and perhaps as despoilers of nature, too, if they ran afoul of the nascent environmental movement. So pervasive was the anti-corporate bias in popular culture that Mike Nichols' 1967 film *The Graduate* could condemn an entire industry with a single word: "Plastics."

Business had done itself no favors either. In generally prosperous times, it had managed to self-destruct in its relationships with government, its losing struggle with the solitary Ralph Nader, its negotiating posture with labor, its general public image, and its repulsion of the most talented youth. No doubt about it, business needed a godfather with connections in the highest councils to look out for its interests and a consigliere to point it in the right direction. In Lewis F. Powell Jr. it got both.

Lewis Powell is both a figure of traditional virtues and a virtual prototype of conventional success. Born into a well-off family in Suffolk, Virginia, he was educated at private schools and later at staunchly conservative Washington & Lee University and Harvard Law School, from which he earned his degree in 1931. After his marriage to Josephine Rucker, the daughter of a leading Richmond physician, Powell moved into his in-laws' antebellum mansion and began climbing up the ranks at Hunton & Williams, by far the most establishment law firm in establishment-oriented Virginia.

In time, Powell became the most respected and sought-after lawyer in the state, and one of the most admired attorneys in the country. At various intervals, he served as president of both the American Bar Association and the American College of Trial Lawyers, no mean accomplishments for a man of modest appetites. In Richmond, as is expected of Hunton & Williams's best and brightest, Powell became a vital force in civic affairs. But it was in corporate and securities law, that he made his true mark.

Like other states, Virginia had over the years enacted a paraphernalia of laws and regulatory structure under which corporations chartered in the state were required to function; and from the end of World War II onward for a quarter century, Lewis Powell more than any other attorney in the state was the go-to guy for wending one's way through the maze. Inevitably, perhaps, Powell found himself serving not only as outside counsel for a variety of companies but as a member on their boards of directors as well.

To suspicious eyes, this dual relationship might suggest an unacceptable conflict of interest. Will not a lawyer, serving as director, inevitably make decisions that are in the particular interest of his law firm even when they might not serve the best interest of the company? At the least, wouldn't Powell's training and proclivities incline him toward legal solutions that would in the end redound to his own benefit and to the benefit of Hunton & Williams?

Those are probably insoluble issues. The law makes life meaningful for lawyers in the same way that surgery makes life meaningful for surgeons. It is the prism—and the bias— through which they see the world. Besides, while recognizing the existence of self-interest, the culture of which Powell was so deeply a part had great faith in the values of "the best people." Of course, there might be conflicts of interest. The recipient of large fees and praise from corporate enterprise might be unlikely to expend much energy—certainly no public energy—in introspection about the niceties of corporate governance. Nevertheless, those in a position of authority could be trusted to make the right choices, and the purpose of governance and law was to support their capacity to do so.

As A. C. Pritchard wrote in a March 2003 article for the *Duke Law Journal:*

> Powell's nearly 40 years of experience in corporate board rooms led him to trust the character of the average American businessman. That trust was reinforced by working alongside those clients in civic affairs. In Powell's world, free enterprise and the businessmen who made it work were the foundation of strong communities. Free enterprise was a resource to be preserved, not a menace to be tamed. Character, not the threat of lawsuits, was the safeguard of the integrity of American capitalism. That trust in American business led Powell to read the securities laws—in all good faith—as setting down predictable rules that would allow business to proceed without undue interference or liability risk.

Lewis Powell was smart. He was connected. He knew business inside and out—as director and legal counsel. When he looked over the social and political landscape of the late 1960s and early 1970s, he saw the same deteriorating conditions that other executives and board members saw. Unlike many others, though, Powell didn't stop with wringing his hands over matters or complaining about them in the sanctity of the nineteenth hole. On August 23, 1971, Powell sent his client, the chairman of the Education Committee of the U.S. Chamber of Commerce, a blistering and penetrating 6,466-word analysis of the present defensive posture of business in American society and recommendations to improve it.

Under the title "Confidential Memorandum: Attack of American Free Enterprise System," Powell lays into all the usual suspects of the time: New Leftists, old statists, academic rabble-rousers like Yale's Charles Reich, lawyer-firebrands such as William Kuntsler—the whole Hate-and-Blame America crowd and the media that, according to Powell, exaggerates the Left's importance while denying microphones to responsible voices from the Right.

Yet, as Powell writes, "The most disquieting voices joining the chorus of criticism come from perfectly respectable elements of society: from the college campus, the pulpit, the media, the intellectual and literary journals, the arts and sciences, and from politicians." Even more disquieting was the tacit capitulation of business to its own sworn enemies:

> One of the bewildering paradoxes of our time is the extent to which the enterprise system tolerates, if not participates in, its own destruction. The campuses from which much of the criticism emanates are supported by (a) tax funds generated largely from American business, and (b) contributions from capital funds controlled or generated by American business. The boards of trustees of our universities overwhelmingly are composed of men and women who are leaders in the system. Most of the media, including the national TV systems, are owned and theoretically controlled by corporations which depend upon profits, and the enterprise system to survive.

Having reminded business that it did, in fact, hold the ultimate power of the purse, Powell went on to lay out an aggressive "education" program, including assemblages of scholars and speakers to counter the dogma of the New Left, the aggressive evaluation of textbooks and of TV network news broadcasts, demands for equal time on campus and for more ideologically balanced faculties. As Powell noted, "This is a long road and not one for the fainthearted." In his memo, Powell envisions these scholars and textbook-and-media sleuths acting under the aegis of a newly aggressive

U.S. Chamber of Commerce. Instead, upstart "think tanks" such as the Heritage Foundation and Cato Institute seemed to take up Powell's call to arms, and his agenda.

Education, however, was only part of the answer, the slow route to the desired counterrevolution in public opinion. What Powell called the "neglected political arena" was where the action waited.

"As every business executive knows, few elements of American society today have as little influence in government as the American businessman, the corporation, or even the millions of corporate stockholders. If one doubts this, let him undertake the role of 'lobbyist' for the business point of view before Congressional committees. The same situation obtains in the legislative halls of most states and major cities. One does not exaggerate to say that, in terms of political influence with respect to the course of legislation and government action, the American business executive is truly the 'forgotten man.'"

Powell goes on in the memo to lament the "impotency" of business and the herd mentality of politicians who cavil to the consumerist and environmental movements while ignoring or, worse, dismissing out of hand the corporations that provide "the goods, services and jobs on which our country depends." Education, he writes, will help level the playing field against such formidable and formidably ignorant and deluded foes, but education is not in itself enough.

"Business must learn the lesson, long ago learned by labor and other self-interest groups. This is the lesson that political power is necessary; that such power must be assiduously cultivated; and that when necessary, it must be used aggressively and with determination—without embarrassment and without the reluctance which has been so characteristic of American business."

Just as it is a stretch to credit Powell with being the progenitor of Heritage, Cato, and other think tanks of the right, it is probably overstatement to credit him with the vast expansion of lobbyists and corporate involvement in politics over the 35 years since he wrote, but his words were as important as any other single factor. At the least, every man and woman who heads up the Washington office of a Fortune 500 company should say a little prayer to Powell on the way to bed at night.

As events turned out, Powell's most prescient comments were reserved for another "neglected opportunity"—the courts. Noting that "liberal" and "far left" organizations such as the American Civil Liberties Union, labor unions, civil-rights groups, and the new public-interest law firms had made free use of the courts, including the Supreme Court, in their collective assault on American business, Powell urged business and the Chamber to fight back through the courts as well.

"This is a vast area of opportunity for the Chamber," he writes in the memo, "if it is willing to undertake the role of spokesman for American business and if, in turn, business is willing to provide the funds. As with respect to scholars and speakers, the Chamber would need a highly competent staff of lawyers. In special situations it should be authorized to engage, to appear as counsel amicus in the Supreme Court, lawyers of national standing and reputation. The greatest care should be exercised in selecting the cases in which to participate, or the suits to institute. But the opportunity merits the necessary effort."

Two months later, on October 20, 1971, President Richard Nixon nominated Lewis Powell to fill the Supreme Court seat vacated by Hugo Black's retirement. Although the lengthy Chamber memo in which Powell derided so many politicians as essentially New Left lackeys was leaked to the muckraking columnist Jack Anderson, it never surfaced at his nomination hearing in any significant way. Nor was there any meaningful consideration of the fact that

Powell had spent his professional lifetime in the employ of corporate powers. By contrast to Nixon's earlier efforts to place southern conservatives Clement Haynsworth and Harold Carswell on the Court, the then 64-year-old Powell seemed both stately and enlightened.

Escorted through the nomination process on what amounted to a red carpet, Lewis Powell was confirmed with ease and took his seat officially on January 7, 1972. Not only had the consigliere gotten his nose under the tent flap; he had been handed a place on the highest bench in the land.

Like many justices, Powell deviated from expectations during his 15 years on the Court. In Richmond, he had broken with the state political establishment over its "massive resistance" to school desegregation. In Washington, he continued to surprise on occasion. To the Nixon administration's displeasure, Powell wrote the majority opinion in the *Bakke* case, allowing college and universities to consider race among other factors in weighing applications for admission. He also sided with the majority in forcing Nixon to turn over the famous Watergate tapes. On the subject of corporate power and its expansion, however, Lewis Powell was steady as she goes.

Corporations are creatures of law, yet the U.S. Constitution never mentions the word "corporation." Indeed, it's only through a backdoor that the notion arose of a corporation having any constitutional status or protection. The Fourteenth Amendment to the Constitution, ratified in July 1868, provided, among other measures, "due process of law" to the newly freed slaves of the recently defeated South. History all but required such a measure. It wasn't long, though, before corporate lawyers seized on the new amendment to claim constitutional protection not only for flesh-and-blood human beings but for corporations as well.

The Supreme Court seemed to agree in its decision in an 1886 case, *Santa Clara County v. Southern Pacific Railroad*, but "seemed" is the key word. The Court's approving nod is found in handwritten notes on the oral arguments in the case, not in the decision itself.

This interpretation of a corporation as a "legal person" has never been expressly adopted, nor has it been expressly overruled. Successive courts have simply treated it as a reality. It was Powell more than any other justice who shaped the interpretation and gave teeth to the nonperson person that the Fourteenth Amendment had perhaps created. In his majority opinions in two cases, Powell both created "corporate speech" and affirmed management's full discretion in determining exactly what such "speech" would entail.

In a 1978 case, *First National Bank of Boston v. Bellotti*, a 5 to 4 majority led by Powell upheld the claims of a First Amendment right for corporations to influence ballot questions. As Powell famously put it: "The inherent worth of the speech in terms of its capacity for informing the public does not depend upon the identity of its source, whether corporation, association, union or individual." In so arguing, Powell created, almost literally out of his own mind, a constitutional right of "corporate speech," access to which the public could not be deprived.

In his dissent to the majority opinion, Justice William Rehnquist saw clearly both the potential impact of protected "corporate speech" and the spurious reasoning behind it. As Rehnquist wrote:

A state grants to a business corporation the blessings of potentially perpetual life and limited liability to enhance its efficiency as an economic entity. It might reasonably be concluded that those properties, so beneficial in the economic sphere, pose special dangers in the political sphere.

Furthermore, it might be argued that liberties of political expression are not at all necessary to effectuate the purposes for which States permit commercial corporations to exist. So long as the Judicial Branches of the State and Federal Governments remain open to protect the corporation's interest in its property, it has no need, though it may have the desire, to petition the political branches for similar protection. Indeed, the States might reasonably fear that the corporation would use its economic power to obtain further benefits beyond those already bestowed.

Such concerns apparently did not trouble Justice Powell. Nor was he troubled when he bestowed on corporate management the right to censor its critics. In 1986, in *Pacific Gas & Electric v. Public Utilities Commission,* writing for a 5 to 3 majority, Powell held that a public utility company was not obligated to include in its billing envelope a consumer group's quarterly newsletter, even when the newsletter would not increase postage costs or otherwise economically inconvenience the mailer. Eight years earlier, in *Bellotti,* Powell had discovered a constitutional protection for all corporate speech; now he uncovered congruent constitutional protection for corporate management not to be associated with views it disagreed with. As Ted Nace wrote in *Gangs of America: The Rise of Corporate Power and the Disabling of Democracy,* "To give First Amendment protection to an official newsletter while denying it to a rate-payer newsletter, an employee newsletter, or a stockholder newsletter is in effect to grant constitutional protection to management over and above other groups involved with the corporation."

During Powell's last year on the Court, he again played a key role in protecting management prerogatives, this time in a decision about the constitutionality of state laws preventing hostile takeovers. The rise of junk bonds in the late 1970s and early 1980s and the spectacular success of Michael Milken had turned hostile takeovers from a relatively rare event to almost a commonplace one. To stem the tide and to protect local corporations, state legislatures had enacted a raft of hasty antitakeover measures that were mostly voided by the Court in a 1982 decision. Second-generation antitakeover laws were more sophisticated, however; and five years later, with Powell writing the majority opinion, the Court reversed itself in an Indiana-based case, *CTS Corporation v. Dynamics Corp of America.*

In an internal memorandum written during arguments, Powell spelled out his position. Legislation enabling the takeover craze, he wrote, "has become an economic disaster—a view that increasingly is being held by responsible economists. Indeed, hearings are now pending in the Congress to consider appropriate means of curbing takeover bids, and the bypassing in effect of antitrust laws." Predictably, Powell's thinking carried the day. Justices have a tradition of deferring to one another in their areas of expertise. Not only was Powell the Court's acknowledged authority on corporate law; his fellow justices were for the most part surprisingly ignorant of basic business principles.

For sitting management, Powell's opinion and the subsequent "Powell proof" legislation enacted by many states was a gift from above. For the free-enterprise system Powell professes to love, however, the justice's "gift" was anything but. Hostile or not, the possibility of takeover is the prime weapon of ownership in requiring accountability from management. Put in economic terms, ultimate protection of the principal against abuse by the agent lies in the capacity of free bidders to acquire an underperforming company. Henceforth, thanks to Powell and those who voted with him, American shareholders would no longer have this power in unabridged form. Thus the ultimate restraint on management entrenchment was weakened and in some cases removed altogether.

No one contends that Lewis Powell was anything other than supremely competent, least of all me. Only weeks before his nomination to the Supreme Court, I contacted Powell about representing me in a civil matter. Just about everyone who followed corporate law knew he was the best in the business. No one that I know of argues convincingly that Powell set out to line his own pockets or those of his corporate friends with his decisions. As a justice, Powell acted as he had in his lawyer days—on principle based on deep conviction. For my part, I doubt that he could even begin to foresee the modern corporate hegemony that his decisions would do so much to create. Powell's reference points were the Great Depression and the New Left uprisings of the 1960s and 1970s. In his own mind, he was restoring a lost balance, not tipping the scales heavily in business's favor. But the fact remains that the unrestrained creatures Powell helped so significantly to create are with us still.

Justice Powell provided the juridical framework that has allowed management to commit untold corporate resources to *influence* public opinion and public votes— resources so huge and unmatchable that individual contributions are now all but meaningless in state and national elections. His finding of a constitutionally protected right to "corporate speech" almost assures that campaign-funding reform will be more illusory than real no matter which political party is flacking it. Building on Powell's opinions, domiciliary states are free to provide legislative relief against the discipline of hostile takeovers, a corporate protection that grows in value with the incompetence of a CEO and his or her top lieutenants.

With Powell leading the way in turning his trailblazing U.S. Chamber of Commerce memo into the law of the land, all that was necessary to consolidate corporate power was for those who held the bulk of it to pool their resources. The Business Roundtable took care of that.

Chapter Four

THE BUSINESS ROUNDTABLE

One day in late May 2006, John Castellani, the president of the Business Roundtable (BRT), drove out to the Rockville, Maryland, headquarters of Institutional Shareholder Services (ISS) to meet with its CEO, John Connolly. Judging solely by the surface of things, this would not appear to be an extraordinary event. The BRT is headquartered on Rhode Island Avenue in Washington, DC, not more than a half hour away by car or Metro. What's more, the two groups would seem to share common interests.

I founded ISS in 1985 to advise institutional investors on proxy voting and on corporate governance issues. Over more than two decades, much of that time under the innovative ownership of my son, Bobby, ISS has grown into the world's largest such service. Today, it provides some 1,700 clients with proxy analysis, impartial research, and voting recommendations for more than 35,000 companies operating in 115 markets around the world. Although Bobby sold the company in January 2007, the core mission of ISS remains unchanged: to enhance the interaction between shareholders and companies and to help shareholders manage risk and drive value.

The Business Roundtable is older than ISS by 13 years and has far deeper pockets. Formed in 1972 out of the merger of three preexisting organizations, the BRT limits its membership to CEOs of leading companies. Among its

160 members are the heads of Aetna, Alcoa, Allstate, American Express, Archer Daniels Midland, and on and on. Past chairmen of the group have included Phil Condit of Boeing; John Dillon of International Paper; John Snow of CXS, later to be George W. Bush's second Treasury secretary; Drew Lewis of Union Pacific, who had earlier served as Ronald Reagan's Secretary of Transportation; all the way back to the founding chairman, W. B. Murphy of Campbell Soup. One doesn't need to go beyond the first letter of the alphabet or list every chairman to understand that BRT has considerable clout in corporate America.

Inevitably, tensions arise between the two groups. ISS represents owners, especially the institutional shareholders who tend to be most involved in their ownership stakes. BRT speaks for management, in particular its very top tier. Whatever the endeavor, ownership and management do not always get along, but with business, the common goals—greater profit, better governance, increased shareholder value, good corporate citizenship—are so manifest and plentiful that one might expect natural rivalries to be subsumed by larger matters. Between Institutional Shareholder Services and the Business Roundtable, though, that has rarely been the case. John Castellani had never visited ISS before, and when he did this time, he wasn't paying a courtesy call.

Castellani had driven—or more likely had been driven—the roughly 20 miles between the two headquarters so he could berate John Connolly for ISS's recommendation that Pfizer shareholders withhold their proxy votes from compensation committee members who were involved in approving the pay package for CEO Henry McKinnell. The fact that McKinnell was doubling at the time as chairman of the Business Roundtable undoubtedly stoked Castellani's fire, but Connolly was not a man to suffer insult lightly.

"Are you threatening me?" he asked Castellani.

"No," the artful BRT head replied. "I'm giving you a message."

Again looking solely at the surface of things, this would seem to be an unusual mission for John Castellani to undertake, even given that he was essentially working at the time for McKinnell. When I last checked its website, the BRT listed eight task forces: Corporate Governance; Education & the Workforce; Fiscal Policy; Environment, Technology, & the Economy; Energy; Health & Retirement; International Trade & Investment; and Security. None would appear to have as its purview executive compensation.

Similarly, a full-page ad available for downloading from the website is mute on the subject of CEO pay. "Roundtable member companies make significant contributions to the economy, to society, and to the world," the ad proclaims, by:

- Strengthening the Economy
- Making a Difference in the World
- Providing Value to Shareholders
- Supporting a Strong National Infrastructure
- Leading Innovation and Research

A quick glance at the ad and at BRT's mission as portrayed on its website would suggest the Roundtable is almost a philanthropic organization. "Roundtable companies give more than $7 billion a year in combined charitable contributions, representing nearly 60 percent of total corporate giving," according to the website. "They are technology innovation leaders, with $90 billion in annual research and development spending—nearly half of the total private R&D spending in the United States." None of this is exactly tithing or even surprising. The 160 member companies account for $4.5 trillion in annual revenues, employ some 10 million people, and comprise more than a third of the total value of all U.S. stock markets. Still, one looks in vain for any mention of CEO compensation.

What then was John Castellani's message? And why had he made this unprecedented trip to ISS's Rockville, Maryland, headquarters to deliver it? The answer to those questions goes to the heart of why the Business Roundtable really exists—its stealth core mission as opposed to its public one.

Whether the Business Roundtable is the direct spawn of Lewis Powell's August 1971 memo to the Education Director of the U.S. Chamber of Commerce is open to question. Although the group was founded within a year of the memo's distribution, BRT claims no direct lineage in its brief online history. No one could doubt, however, that something like BRT is exactly what Powell was hoping for.

Much of the public back then looked out at the landscape of Corporate America and saw price fixing, incipient monopolies, or at worst, maybe, the global collusion of military, government, and business interests supposedly represented by the Trilateral Commission. The reality, though, was starkly different. Big Business was on the whole a clumsy, uncomfortable, and ineffective player in American politics. Far from dictating its wishes to Congress, the presidency, and regulatory bodies, U.S. corporations had proved strikingly inept at exerting power or even influence over their rule makers. Whether it was General Motors getting caught hiring a private detective to deal with Ralph Nader in the 1960s or the Big-Business-backed Richard Nixon declaring himself a Keynesian and using his presidency to go off the gold standard and impose wage and price controls, the evidence of faux pas, maddening frustrations, and multitudinous snafus abounded.

The Business Roundtable changed all that. By limiting its membership to CEOs—deputies were not acceptable at meetings or in committee work—and by requiring committee chairs to provide their own staff, the group assured that its physical presence in Washington would be deceptively small. In fact, Corporate America was committing huge resources and some of the best and most expensive business and legal talent in the country to achieving Big Business's government agenda. Almost inevitably, the plan worked.

Through its own published and widely disseminated studies and via the assiduous courting and sometimes strong-arming of the media, Congress, and the executive branch, BRT succeeded in changing the terms of the debate over the limits on corporate reach and self-determination. Union power and presence withered. Corporations were freed of pension obligations that had once seemed set in concrete. Under the banner of "tort reform" and backed by huge political contributions at the national, state, and even local levels, BRT and its allies managed to paint Corporate America as the victim and those injured and otherwise damaged by corporate neglect as the assailants—a seismic shift that continues to this day. For the past 25 years, the group's task force on corporate governance has been shaping the nation's definition and understanding of that critical term, invariably in ways that entrench management and disempower shareholders.

Most profound, perhaps, the Roundtable's relentless touting of its own membership created a new class of philosopher-kings. Before BRT, CEOs were well-paid but slightly dull monomaniacs focused relentlessly on the bottom line and the business immediately at hand—someone you might ask for a favor but didn't look forward to being seated beside at dinnertime. Now, one felt obliged to listen when a CEO droned on over his (or occasionally her) roast beef about the effectiveness of charters, directors, and boards; the shortcomings of the mainstream media; and the magic mix of economic, legal, and social constraints that would allow a thousand businesses to thrive and create a rising tide to lift all ships.

In another era, people such as Lee Iacocca, Jack Welch, Andy Grove, and Ross Perot might have spent their professional lives largely under the radar. In the new era as defined in great part by BRT's image campaign, they were best-selling authors, revered business theorists, presidential timber. The New Left still had a place at the table—it didn't disappear overnight—but its seat was likely now to be below the salt, often far below, just as Lewis Powell had envisioned in his Chamber memo.

As never before in American life, CEOs had come of age, not just politically but in the public's estimation, and the message they delivered was remarkably consistent: Unleash us, free Big Business from crippling legal and regulatory restraints, allow us to compete unimpeded on the global frontier, and the American economy shall prosper as never before. In large part, that has happened. The fetters were thrown off. Lofty environmental goals were rolled back or scratched altogether. State legislatures capped punitive damages. Coincidentally or not, the stock market boomed, went bust, then boomed again. But what the CEOs were really interested in doing, it seems, was unleashing their own pay from any standards of restraint: accounting, moral, or otherwise.

The outlines of the CEO raid on the U.S. corporate treasuries have been widely broadcast. To cite some of the most obvious examples, in 1970, two years before BRT came into existence, the average CEO earned less than 30 times the average wage of all production workers. Today, that gap has grown 10-fold, to 300 times the average worker's pay, more than double the gap in the 13 other richest nations. Between 1990 and 2005, the 10 highest paid U.S. CEOs brought home an aggregate $11.7 billion in total compensation—salary, bonuses, restricted stock awards, payouts on long-term incentives, and the value of options exercised over the 15-year time frame. From 1996 to 2001, as the high-tech-driven stock market first bubbled, then burst, the richest 1 percent of Americans garnered over 20 percent of all gains in national income.

Total compensation does not include the lavish retirement and severance packages routinely granted departing CEOs at larger U.S. corporations by their starstruck board members, and also routinely hidden from the public record. The $210-million package that Robert Nardelli carried away from Home Depot in early January 2007 was certainly an extreme example of the largesse, but it was only atypical by a factor of maybe two or three, not twenty or fifty as might be the case in a more sane environment.

Nor does total compensation even begin to touch the raid on shareholder value that routinely occurs when one corporate behemoth gets folded into or bought out by another. Bank of America's $35-billion purchase of MBNA in early 2006 reportedly earned MBNA CEO Bruce Hammond a one-time windfall of $102 million. That works out to $51 million a year for the two years Hammond spent at the helm of the faltering credit-card giant. The generosity didn't stop at the very top either. Former FBI Director Louis Freeh was rewarded for his four-and-a-half years as MBNA's senior vice chairman with a payout said to be $31 million, enough to buy a parachute spun of real gold.

Officially, the Business Roundtable is alarmed by tales of wretched excess among and beyond its membership. The group's "Principles of Executive Compensation," issued in November 2003, states that CEO pay "should be closely aligned with the long-term interests of stockholders and with corporate goals and strategies" and determined by a "compensation committee composed entirely of independent directors.'' It urges such committees to review maximum payout, including all benefits and under multiple scenarios, and to avail themselves of expertise in the field; and it charges corporations to provide "complete, accurate, understandable, and timely disclosure to stockholders concerning all significant elements of executive compensation and executive compensation practices.''

In practice, BRT does just about everything it can to subvert its own published principles. Paul Hodgson of the Corporate Library has shown how at the very same time the Business Roundtable was proclaiming the "best practice" of full disclosure of compensation arrangements, its chairman, Pfizer's Henry McKinnell, was awarded an unrevealed pension of $5.9 million per year, or even more if he chose to remarry—this for a CEO who had seen the stock price of Pfizer drop 40 percent on his watch.

Nowhere do BRT's actions more belie its words than in the matter of stock options, the stealth bomber of CEO compensation. Like the B-2, they pack an enormous wallop—the preponderance of the billions of dollars paid to CEOs like American Surgical's Leon Hirsch, Coca-Cola's late Roberto Goizueta, Citigroup's Sanford Weill, and Disney's Michael Eisner over the past decade and a half have come from option profits. Like the herpes virus, an increasing percentage of stock options also never go away. More and more such grants come with a reloading feature. Once the CEO exercises an option, he or she is automatically granted further options for the same number of shares as were used to pay for the exercise. The public logic is that, this way, the CEO's interests are kept in constant alignment with the interests of shareholders. The private logic is more straightforward: If the board is going to keep putting gold back in the mine once it's depleted, why not keep taking it out?

An ISS study found that, in 1992, the top 15 individuals in each company received 97 percent of the stock options issued to all employees. *BusinessWeek* has calculated that the 200 largest corporations set aside nearly 10 percent of their stock for top executives, and especially for the super-star CEOs who make up BRT's membership. Far more dangerous, option obligations are almost impossible to track on any continuing basis because corporations are not required to carry them on the balance sheet as year-by-year liabilities. In effect, it's simply understood they will be made good on whenever the options kick in.

Though this situation is absurd on its face, even modest efforts at reform have been met by the BRT with the same ferocity that the National Rifle Association reserves for, say, legislation that might make it a felony to carry a loaded Uzi onto a school playground. Caught up in a wave of public concern in the early 1990s over CEO compensation, the Financial Accounting Standards Board (FASB) revived a dormant recommendation that corporations record the fair value of options and charge them against earnings, like other compensation expenses, at the time of grant. By not making such a charge, said FASB and other critics, CEOs were in effect paying themselves under-the-table compensation.

Rather than deal with this argument on its merits, the Roundtable developed a comprehensive and ultimately successful strategy to protect its members' wallets by silencing their critics. Citicorp chairman John Reed, who was then serving as chairman of the BRT's accounting principles task force, first learned about the proposed changes for stock-option accounting in early 1992, in a meeting with FASB executives. Joined by Bruce Atwater and several other BRT members, he set out to rally BRT members to take suitable steps to deal with the problem. In a June 23, 1992, letter sent out on the organization's stationery to all BRT members, Reed wrote:

We need help from BRT CEOs in the following areas:

1. Communication with and education of your public accountants.
2. Communication with and education of your compensation consultants.
3. Communication with FASB now, before their views become solidified.

We believe these contacts would be most effective if made by CEOs.

In BRT-speak, "communication" and "education" take on an almost Orwellian cast. On the whole, the large accounting firms did not need great encouragement to come around to Big Business's side on stock options or much of anything else. By the mid-1990s, the once skeptical bean counters at places like Arthur Andersen and Ernst & Young had already migrated a long way toward becoming corporate consultants whose main responsibility was not to make sure the books balanced and all liabilities were duly recorded but rather to help corporate management "explain itself to investors," as John C. Coffee Jr. put in his 2006 study *Gatekeepers: The Role of the Professions in Corporate Governance.* Even today, and despite the Sarbanes-Oxley legislation that was supposed to fix such things, management retains complete discretion over the choice of accounting principles, thus almost assuring future catastrophic implosions like the ones that brought down Enron and WorldCom.

"Communicating" with and "educating" FASB on the errors of its position that stock options should be charged against earnings was a harder sell, but not an impossible one. Timothy S. Lucas, the now-retired research director of FASB, told the *New York Times* about being summoned along with the Board's voting members to a meeting at Reed's

Citicorp office. In the past, Lucas said, FASB had tried in vain to involve CEOs in their deliberations. Now that options were on the table, they couldn't keep them out of it. Reed was joined for the meeting by Jack Welch of GE and Sandy Weill, then head of Travelers Group. Together, this all-star chorus sang the praises of stock options. They were an excellent motivational tool, part of the engine of the economic dynamism that was roaring through the American economy. FASB's proposed rule change would ruin the party, its board members were told. Companies would no longer be willing to issue stock options if they had to count them on the balance sheet. Lucas recalled leaving the meeting with the distinct understanding that even if FASB did go ahead with its new rule, the SEC would never enforce it. Big Business was too opposed. In any event, the showdown never came. FASB backed away.

Just to be certain the idea didn't rear up from some other, unexpected angle, BRT and its allies prevailed on Connecticut Senator Joe Leiberman and 15 cosponsors to introduce a "sense of the Senate" amendment stating that "the Financial Accounting Standards Board should maintain the current accounting treatment of employee stock options and employee stock purchase plans." On May 3, 1994, the Senate agreed to the amendment by an 88 to 9 voice vote. When it comes to protecting stock options, there is no such thing as overkill.

BRT moved with equal determination to quash a shareholder-access rule proposed by the Securities and Exchange Commission (SEC) in the fall of 2003. Backed by institutional investors, a wide spread of corporate governance experts, and even by SEC Chairman William Donaldson, the rule would have lowered the barriers erected to keep shareholders from placing their own nominees on a company's board of directors. At best, this was a modest effort at reform that addressed the wrong end of the problem. There would be no need to suggest shareholder nominations of directors if American shareholders, like those virtually everywhere else in the western world, had the absolute right to call a meeting at which a majority of those present could remove with or without cause any or all directors. That is leverage, and the pressure is at the right point. Modest as the proposed access rule was, though, CEOs opposed it with typical vengeance and overkill. Over the 18 months beginning in January 2003, BRT spent nearly $13 million lobbying federal officials, much of that on stopping the proposed SEC rule. The U.S. Chamber of Commerce lent its weight in opposition, as did Treasury Secretary Snow, a former Roundtable chairman. In time, Donaldson backed off, just as FASB had.

Like BRT and in lockstep with it, the U.S. Chamber of Commerce opposes giving shareholders any meaningful access. Michael Ryan, head of the Chamber's "Competitiveness Center," is on record as questioning whether the SEC has the basic authority to allow changes such as those outlined previously and more recent efforts to reform the voting of "broker shares," which are all but automatically cast for management, and to ease the process by which shareholders can nominate candidates for the board of directors, a possibility both the Chamber and BRT seem to equate roughly to Original Sin. Split between two Democratic and two Republican commissioners; led by a Republican-appointed Chairman, former Congressman Christopher Cox; and hammered constantly by BRT, the Chamber, and related groups, the SEC today exudes dysfunctionality.

When it came to protecting stock options, the Business Roundtable communicated with and educated compensation consultants much as it had the accounting regulators. Those BRT members who were clients of Towers Perrin, one of the largest such consultants, convinced it to cease helping the *Wall*

Street Journal prepare its annual executive pay survey. Slow to get the message or too dense to understand it, four other consulting firms and one of the major accounting outfits did comply with a technical request from FASB, asking them to demonstrate how they would value five types of stock options. When all five complied, several BRT chief executives expressed extreme displeasure that the consultants had undermined BRT's contention that values cannot easily be placed on options. And with that, the discussion died down to less than a murmur. Upsetting your biggest clients might be occasionally good for the conscience, but it's almost always bad for business.

How the George W. Bush administration stood on executive compensation became abundantly clear in late 2002 when John Snow was nominated to replace Paul O'Neill as secretary of the Treasury. As CEO of the CSX rail system from 1996 to 2001, Snow had been effectively loaned more than $27 million against the future worth of stock awarded him by his board. CSX stock, though, performed poorly during Snow's tenure. By the target date, the future Treasury secretary's stock was worth only $17 million, a shortfall of serious dimension, but never mind. The CSX board canceled the option deal, saving Snow from having to pay back the $10 million difference out of his own pocket, and awarded him a further $4.3 million in stock and other incentives. Not only were CEOs to be "incentivized" with stock; they were to be protected from any risk when they underperformed and their stock deals went sour, and from any public opprobrium either. At Snow's confirmation hearing to be Treasury secretary, Iowa Republican Chuck Grassley expressly prohibited consideration of the nominee's compensation package because, as Grassley put it, "this is the prevailing pattern."

The Business Roundtable excuses the compensation rapaciousness of its members as the mere playing out of free-market forces at work. Look at pro basketball. Look at pro baseball. Look at Hollywood. If you want to run with the wolves, you have to be prepared to turn the purse inside out. Yet even a cursory examination of the numbers says otherwise.

Compare the compensation paid to two successive generations of CEOs of Exxon, generally accepted as a market leader. In 1993, Lawrence Rawl received $14,828,873 in realizable equity, including an annual pension of $1,465,600. That works out to $1,508 per hour. In 2005, in the same position, Lee Raymond earned, if that's even the right word, compensation at the rate of $34,457 per hour, including an annual pension of $8,187,200, for a total realizable equity of $252,744,480—16.25 times more than Rawl was paid a dozen years earlier. In retirement, Raymond also was guaranteed a one-time, annual consultancy fee of $1,000,000 and, for two years, continued provision of a residential security system, personal security personnel, a car and personal security driver, business and personal use of ExxonMobil aircraft as well as Exxon office space and administrative assistants valued at $200,000. Rawl, who died in 2005, retired with a pension and no other benefits, or at least none that were disclosed (see Table 4.1).

Although Exxon is a larger company in 2005 than it was in 1993 and Raymond has been a manager of conspicuous ability, there can be no suggestion that his pay is based on the proposition that his service was 16 times more valuable than that of Rawl. This is compensation for its own sake, unmoored from reality.

This same pattern is present in the preponderance of S&P 500 companies. The fundamental economic circumstances include a very high level of compensation at the beginning of the period, no diminution in the number of qualified individuals to serve as CEO during this period, no increase in the required skills or risks implicit in performing the job—in brief, no change in the market for CEOs. And yet

Table 4.1   Comparison of Exxon CEO Compensation

Compensation	Lawrence Rawl (1993)	Lee Raymond (2005)
Hourly wage	$1,508	$34,457
Total compensation in final year of employment	$2,929,056	$70,134,830
Maximum earnings bonus-unit plan payout	$250,000	$4,900,500
Estimated annual pension	$1,465,600	$8,187,200
Realizable equity at retirement	$14,828,873	$252,744,480
Annual consultancy fee	Not applicable	$1,000,000
Postretirement benefits	Not disclosed	Less than $1,000,000 (company estimate)

BRT and its members keep rolling out this same perceived "need to meet the competition" to justify the stratospheric rise in compensation. The market is static. It is the pay that has shot through the roof along with the willingness to take it in the absence of any need. Shareholder value is being looted solely because it exists in such abundance and because shareholders are for the most part powerless to stop the looting. This is the hallmark not of a democracy but of a *kleptocracy*, the sort of grab-all that conquering armies like so much.

Even if you make the basis of comparison the sharp rise in sales and profits since the early 1990s, the numbers don't hold up. A study conducted by Lucian Bebchuk of Harvard and Cornell's Yaniv Grinstein analyzed multiple factors including profits, company size, and product mix to predict how much executive compensation would have risen over the 10 years beginning in 1993 if it had been pegged to bottom-line performance. Their conclusion: 1,500 publicly traded companies had overpaid their top brass a collective (and staggering) $8.7 billion in 2003, excluding bloated pensions and other incentives.

The simple fact is that the CEO market that the Business Roundtable loves to cite was contrived by the chief executive officers operating through their lobbying wing. It is a market that has been polluted by the secrecy that surrounds the cost of option grants, the lack of any disclosure of even the most enormous retirement benefits, and, recently, the obfuscation of the dates when options were granted and became effective so as to fix a price. Thus rigged and polluted, the market has been sustained by the raw exercise of power: the often unchallenged dominance of CEOs over their boards and compensation committees, the cynical use of compensation consultants, the compromising of the accounting profession, and the unmanning of legislative and regulatory watchdogs. Begun ostensibly as an organization to advance the interests of large companies, BRT has come to function in significant part as an agent for the CEOs who head up those companies. Through BRT and thanks to its efforts, the big-corporation CEOs have established themselves as a new and separate class in the governance of American corporations, answerable to virtually no one, accountable only to themselves. Not even the Medicis had it any better than this.

Where will it end? I don't pretend to know, but given the unwillingness and perhaps—in practical political terms— the inability of the SEC to step forward on behalf of shareholders, it seems almost certain the courts will have to be involved sooner or later if investors are ever going to regain the prerogatives that should rightfully be theirs.

Since I trained and practiced as a lawyer, and since this chapter began with John Castellani's delivering a message on behalf of Business Roundtable chairman and Pfizer CEO Henry McKinnell, I am ending it with my own message on the same subject. Although I have the standing to bring such a legal action—Ram Trust Services manages a significant position in Pfizer stock—the suit as presented here is theoretical only. Were it real, I might have filed it in May 2006, just after John Castellani's visit. Instead, I was still working on the details a few months later when Pfizer's board approved a $198 million payout for McKinnell and sent him packing after five dismal years on the job. While that required me to recast parts of this in the past tense, it also proved that the need for a legal action of this sort is greater than ever.

United States District Court
District of Connecticut
Ram Trust Services, for and on Behalf of
Pfizer, Inc., Plaintiff
v.
Henry A. McKinnell, Defendant

Complaint
Shareholder Derivative Action
Jury Trial Demanded

Plaintiff, Ram Trust Services, hereby institutes this Derivative Action on behalf of and for the benefit of Pfizer, Inc. (Pfizer), pursuant to F.R.Civ. P. 23.1 against Defendant, Henry A. McKinnell Jr., alleging as follows:

Jurisdiction, Venue, and Jury Trial Demand

1. Plaintiff is a Corporation with a principal place of business in Portland, Maine. Plaintiff is the owner of 101,000 shares of the common capital stock of Pfizer. Plaintiff acquired shares in Pfizer prior to the year 2000 and has owned them continuously ever since. Plaintiff owned shares of Pfizer at the time of the transaction of which complaint is here made and has owned them continuously ever since. This action is not a collusive one to confer jurisdiction on a court of the United States, which it would not otherwise have.

2. Defendant is a resident of Greenwich, Connecticut. Defendant formerly served as the president and chief executive officer of Pfizer, Inc., a Delaware corporation with a principal place of business in New York City, New York (Pfizer). Pfizer does business in each of the 50 American states, including Connecticut, and in many nations of the world.

3. This action is brought by Plaintiff on behalf of Pfizer against Pfizer's former chief executive officer. Plaintiff alleges that Defendant conspired with members of Pfizer's board of directors and with chief executive officers of other publicly owned corporations to fix the level of CEO compensation in restraint of the interstate and nationwide market of CEO compensation, and thereby enabled Defendant to garner from Pfizer compensation for his services as Pfizer's CEO

in gross excess of the level of compensation provided by a free market for CEO services.

4. This is a complaint for treble damages and attorneys' fees brought under the Clayton Antitrust Act (15 U.S.C. §15) (Clayton Act). This court has jurisdiction of the claims set forth herein by virtue of 15 U.S.C. §15(a). This court has jurisdiction over the Defendant by virtue of 28 U.S.C. 1691. Venue in this District is proper under 28 U.S.C. §1401. Plaintiff demands trial by jury.

Shareholder Derivative Status

5. Plaintiff brings this action on behalf of Pfizer, which has suffered damage by reason of the conspiracy in restraint of trade herein alleged and set forth. Plaintiff is prepared to maintain this action for the benefit of Pfizer and its entire body of shareholders. Plaintiff has not made demand on the board of directors of Pfizer for the prosecution of this claim because such demand would obviously be futile.

Operative Facts—Liability

6. Pfizer is engaged in the business of manufacture, distribution, and sale of pharmaceutical drugs. It is a "publicly owned corporation" in that no individual shareholder owns more than 5 percent of its outstanding stock. Like all publicly owned corporations, Pfizer is directed by a board of directors (Board). During the period under question, the following individuals served on Pfizer's Board:

> Robert N. Burt
> W. Don Cornwell
> Dana G. Mead
> Ruth J. Simmons
> William C. Steere Jr.
> Michael S. Brown
> Constance J. Horner
> George A. Lorch
> M. Anthony Burns
> Stanley O. Ikenberry
> William H. Gray III

William R. Howell
Defendant, Henry A. McKinnell Jr.
Paul A. Marks
Harry P. Kamen
John F. Niblack
Alex J. Mandl
Franklin D. Raines
Jean-Paul Valles

7. From January 2001 until July 2006, Defendant was Pfizer's chief executive officer (CEO), and from May 2001 until July 2006, Defendant was chairman of Pfizer's Board. Pfizer was then and is still governed "top down" in that the CEO is the head of a team of "management" employees, all of whom report directly or indirectly to the CEO. As CEO, Defendant had the power to direct the activities of all Pfizer employees subject to the general oversight of Pfizer's Board. As CEO, Defendant had the power to hire and fire every Pfizer employee, subject only to the terms of collective bargaining or other contracts, and subject to the general oversight of Pfizer's Board.

8. Under Pfizer's corporate charter, candidates for the Board are nominated by Pfizer management and are then elected by Pfizer shareholders. Defendant and his subordinate management team had the exclusive power to nominate director candidates. During Defendant's tenure as CEO, he nominated all of Pfizer's directors for election or reelection to the Board. No Pfizer director was nominated other than by Pfizer management. Pfizer's corporate charter does not permit any party other than Pfizer management to nominate persons to serve on Pfizer's Board. Although those Directors who are not employed by Pfizer are denominated "independent," in reality no director is independent (i.e., every director owed his or her position to the goodwill of Defendant and his management team while Defendant served as CEO).

9. From his nomination and election as Pfizer's CEO in 2001 until his departure in July 2006, Defendant systematically conspired and combined with diverse other individuals, including the members of Pfizer's Board and the CEOs of other American publicly owned corporations, to extract from

Pfizer and its shareholders compensation and emoluments for his services as CEO far in excess of the compensation and emoluments provided by a free market for CEO services. Such conspiracy within the Pfizer Board was facilitated by the circumstances that:

    a. Directors Burt, Mead, Steere, Lorch, Burns, Howell, and Raines were all former CEOs of American publicly owned companies.

    b. Director Cornwell was an active CEO of an American publicly owned company.

    c. One director was the former chairman and CEO of Pfizer.

    d. Defendant was a member of the boards of three other publicly owned corporations and was chair of the compensation committees of two of them.

10. During Defendant's tenure as CEO of Pfizer, the total annual compensation and emoluments paid to him as Pfizer's CEO increased from $1.35 million in 2001 to over $18 million for the calendar year 2005 (including the realized value of options). This increase in compensation was without reference to the reasonable value of Defendant's services as CEO and without reference to the free-market value of CEO services, and was the result of the conspiracy referred to above and further enumerated below.

11. The free-market value of CEO services for business entities such as Pfizer can be ascertained by studying the compensation of CEOs of corporations owned or controlled by shareholders who have the actual power to choose a board of directors that is accountable to the shareholders. Negotiations between the boards of directors of such corporations and CEOs are at arm's length and reflect the free untrammeled market for CEO services. Examples of such corporations are Dexter Shoe Company (owned or controlled by Berkshire Hathaway Corporation, in turn controlled by Warren Buffett), and West Publishing Company (owned by Thomson, Ltd., in turn controlled by the Thomson family). The compensation of CEOs for such free-market corporations ranges from $1 million to $2 million per year, which

can be regarded as the market compensation for CEO services for enterprises comparable to Pfizer.

12. Defendant and the Board members with whom Defendant conspired and combined were facilitated in their conspiracy by the Business Roundtable (BRT), an organization composed of 160 CEOs of American publicly owned corporations. The BRT was founded in 1972 ostensibly with two major goals: (1) to enable chief executives from different corporations to work together to analyze specific issues affecting the economy and business, and (2) to present government and the public with knowledgeable, timely information and with practical, positive proposals for action for the promotion of the interests of American business organizations. In fact, the BRT has been availed of and used by member CEOs of American publicly owned corporations to coordinate their concerted actions to further their own interests and generate for them and favored members of their management teams increased compensation above and beyond what they could expect from the free market in executive compensation. Defendant was chairman of the BRT from November 2003 until July 2006 and was cochairman of the BRT June to November 2003.

13. Defendant, the coconspirator members of Pfizer's Board, and other CEO coconspirators have created various devices to increase CEO compensation far in excess of market levels. One of these devices is the grant of options to purchase stock in the employer corporation at favorable prices. Such prices are often below the market price of the stock at the date of grant and are "one-way streets" permitting the CEOs to realize on the options in the event of an increase in the market price of the company's stock, but not obligating them to purchase in the event of a decrease. It has long been known that the grant of such options entails a real cost to the shareholders of public corporations by diluting their equity and depressing the market for their own shares. Defendant and the BRT have with one voice opposed any meaningful regulation of the practice of granting options to management employees and have thwarted efforts by the Securities and

Exchange Commission and the Financial Accounting Standards Board to require public companies to account for options granted as expense entries on the income statement of public companies.

14. During 2005, Defendant realized $6,240,414 by the exercise of options for the purchase of Pfizer stock garnered in that or previous years. During 2005, Defendant garnered options to purchase a total of 880,000 shares of Pfizer common stock. The award of these options in no way reflected the performance of the company's common stock, which decreased in value during 2005. Such award of options had no relationship to the market for CEO compensation but was the result of the conspiracy in restraint of trade alleged above.

15. Another device used by Defendant to obtain from Pfizer CEO compensation in excess of that required by the market consisted of excessive arrangements for pensions and deferred compensation. During 2005, Defendant received $5,489,400 pursuant to the Pfizer Long-Term Incentive Plan. This sum was excessive and bears no relationship to the market for CEO services, but was the result of the conspiracy alleged above.

16. Defendant's excessive compensation as CEO was not related to any improvement in Pfizer shareholder value. During Defendant's tenure as CEO, the value of Plaintiff's shares in Pfizer decreased by 40 percent.

Relief Sought

17. Pfizer has suffered damage by virtue of the conspiracies alleged above and the resulting excessive payments made to Defendant as compensation and fringe benefits. Such payments reduced Pfizer's assets, imposed on it continuing liabilities, and depressed the market for Pfizer's stock. During Defendant's tenure, the conspiracy alleged above resulted in total payments to Defendant as CEO of $213 million. Of this, at least $200 million is in excess of any applicable market and therefore the product of the unlawful conspiracies alleged above.

WHEREFORE, Plaintiff, Ram Trust Services, demands judgment in favor of Pfizer, Inc. against Defendant, Henry A. McKinnell, in such amount as the court shall determine as the damage suffered by Pfizer, from the conspiracy alleged above, trebled in accord with 15 U.S.C. sec. 15, plus attorneys' fees and costs in accord with said statutory section.

Attorney for Plaintiff, Ram Trust Services

If $200 million is an appropriate approximation of the damages in a McKinnell suit—and that figure doesn't even take into account the $198 million paid to rid Pfizer of his services—then what might be the damages in a more ambitious undertaking such as *United States of America v. The Business Roundtable* as the principal conspirator on behalf of Henry McKinnell and his fellow CEOs? On that score, we actually have some hard figures to go on. Lucian Bebchuk, the indefatigable and courageous Harvard Law School professor, concludes that the top five executives of public companies increased their compensation from 4.7 percent of profits in 1993–1995 to 10.3 percent of profits in 2001–2003. Extrapolating from those figures alone—and ignoring the revelations of stealth compensation in the years since—the level of damages could easily approach a trillion dollars, an amount of money that even a largely complacent U.S. government might find it tempting to go after.

Chapter Five

INSIDE THE CORPOCRACY

What is proper compensation for someone who runs a business with $35 billion in annual revenues? What is fair pay for a CEO who oversees 100,000 workers spread across six continents? How about severance packages for fired CEOs? Should they be capped at, say, seven figures? Aren't most CEOs fired for *non*performance? And what about retirement benefits? Can anyone justify stripping production workers of guaranteed pensions while rewarding the boss with tens of millions of dollars in payouts and perks for the golden years? What's enough? Too much? Obscene?

Given the rising public rage against supposed excessive CEO compensation and the prospect of congressional hearings on the subject now that the Democrats are back in power, one might think that the Business Roundtable and other defenders of the current pay scale would be inclined to fly beneath the radar, but this is not a group to shrink from battle. As I write, a well-orchestrated campaign is underway across the media frontier to convince the doubtful that what's good for CEOs is good for America.

Maybe the most credible voice on the CEOs' side is the *Economist*. Far from being in anyone's pocket, the *Economist* has long been wedded to the notion that markets, like the magical *deus ex machinas* of medieval morality plays, ultimately explain every conundrum. As Edward Carr wrote in the magazine's January 18, 2007, "Survey of Executive Pay," "The lion's share of the executives' bonanza was deserved—in the sense that shareholders got value for the money they handed over. Those sums on the whole bought and motivated the talent that managed businesses during the recent golden age of productivity growth and profits. Many managers have done extremely well over the past few years; but so, too, have most shareholders."

In Carr's version of events, the explosion in compensation at the top of the pay chart has been chiefly the result of a faddish miscalculation: Over the past decade and a half, too many stock options have been awarded on too generous terms to too many CEOs. "That was costly and unwarranted," he writes, "but it stemmed more from foolish accounting and tax policies supercharged by bull-market mania than from a sinister plot hatched in the executive suite."

I respect the argument, the venue in which it appeared, and the source. I even took the author out to a nice lunch to discuss the piece with him. I just don't happen to agree. Carr finds mistakes and impersonal forces determining critical changes in executive compensation. I prefer the Sherlock Holmes approach. When asked how he possibly could have divined the solution to some impenetrable mystery, Holmes answered: "When you have eliminated the impossible, whatever remains, *however improbable*, must be the truth." That has been my approach. I have eliminated all the impossibilities and found that in the end the only credible explanation for skyrocketing CEO pay is the competent, motivated, and highly greedy men who most benefit from it.

God in Heaven did not suddenly decide one day that a CEO was worth 10 times what he was previously worth. This was not something the stork brought. Stock options didn't come about through one of those blinding moments of revelation such as Saul received on the road to Damascus. This money-grab has been engineered by mortal men (and therefore prone to sin) conspiring to bully the scorekeepers—accountants and legislators—so that the frequently functional idiots on captive compensation committees and boards could be induced to "align executive and shareholder interests" (another bankrupt mantra) through the exercise of super-mega grants to those who set the deal in motion in the first place.

That the grants cost nothing on the profit-and-loss statement as long as they are made in the form of options—and that options lead to a positive cash flow since they are an allowable deduction for tax purposes—only sweetens the kitty. The fact that so many CEOs who thus reward themselves have utter contempt for their shareholders serves to lighten the load of conscience they must bear. That, too, couldn't be more convenient.

The James brothers—Jesse and Frank, not Henry and William—could not have planned it any better. Yet the amount of money currently being paid to top CEOs and tipped into their pockets from all other angles is neither the critical issue nor the truly objectionable point. What is most objectionable and alarming is the failure of governance. The illusion is that we have a system of checks and balances that oversees executive compensation and allows market forces to flow through fairly to the paycheck. The reality is that CEOs in essence pay themselves and do so in ways that need not be disclosed or approved by anyone.

For 30 years and more, reformers have been throwing themselves into the battle against executive arrogance and corporate hegemony; yet mostly what we have to show for all our blood, sweat, and tears are tactical successes, moral victories, and at best marginal advances. The Business Roundtable and its allies bend here, they yield there, but on the critical issues that would lead to meaningful change, they never break. Their funds—paid from company coffers—are inexhaustible. Their shock troops—legal, lobbying, and otherwise—are always fresh and well fed. In the long run, I believe the reformers will prevail because we have right on our side, because public markets will collapse if we don't, and because, like many other reformers, I couldn't go on with the fight if I weren't certain that somewhere down the road shareholders will be vested with the basic right to call a meeting and remove directors when necessity so demands. In the short term, though, despite the best efforts of so many good people, management continues to hold virtually all the cards and, in consequence, the governance deficit in America's publicly traded corporations grows, rather than shrinks. Indeed, the reality of that deficit is being confirmed every day in the old-fashioned way, in the marketplace, by the emergence and growth of private equity whose prosperity is based on governance failure in listed companies.

Needless to say, this fact is not widely advertised by the corpocracy. Indeed, if anything, just the opposite would seem to be the case. A flourishing industry has developed for the precise purpose of measuring the corporate governance levels of American companies. Armed with presumably complicated and well-tested methodology and relying heavily on the quantifiable measures favored by economists, this subindustry has created a full panoply of institutional techniques for rating companies based on everything from the age of directors to the frequency of executive meetings. Also available are codes of best practices for directors and for fiduciary shareholders as well as specialized expertise in voting, compensation, and executive recruitment. The breadth of the exploration alone would seem to guarantee the accuracy of the results. How can a rating based on 500 data points be without value?

On closer examination, though, what appears to be a scientific truth starts to look a good deal more like a statistical Potemkin village. The formulas that in theory balance the complicated factors making up corporate governance are never made public. "Trust me" seems to be the operative phrase. But why? In only rare instances, too, are the outfits doing the ratings free of commercial contact with the companies being rated. Far more often, the evaluation process is paid for in its entirety by a corporation that has voluntarily placed itself under the examiner's eye, with all the potential tainting and skewing of results that such a relationship entails. *Consumer Reports* this is not.

Institutional Shareholder Services commissioned a study to determine if any correlation could be found between these corporate governance ratings and the stock-market performance of the companies rated, The answer: No, there was no observable correlation. Rather than judging by absolute standards, as a scientific model should require, the ratings provide a basis for companies to compare themselves with their peers. That's a low bar to be sure, but apparently it's a measure with sufficient value to support an entire service subindustry.

As troubling as the structural impediments to the rating process are, the underlying assumptions are, in their own way, even worse. The relevance of all the assembled data is based on the belief that actual practice closely accords with legally prescribed procedures—the belief, for example, that shareholders elect directors; that the preponderance of directors of publicly traded companies are independent of management; and that these directors appoint independent compensation committees that, in turn, are authorized to engage independent expert consultants. So thoroughly have the rating agencies engrained this gold standard of independence that the stock exchanges now rush to require ever greater percentages of independent directors on boards and on critical committees while Congress passes laws focused on independent audit committees, all of which only serves to perpetuate the illusion that corporate boards are anything other than self-perpetuating bodies in almost every instance selected by and accountable to the CEO.

It is time to get real, and the reality is that shareholders do not elect directors in any sense beyond the ritual of being sent ballot cards on which are placed the same number of names as there are vacancies to be filled. The names have been nominally provided by a committee of the existing board of directors, but there is no record in history of such a committee nominating an individual not specifically acceptable to the chief executive officer. The company sends these ballot cards with the proxy statement to all shareholders some weeks before the Annual Meeting. Anyone whose name does not appear on the ballot card and who wants to contend for a board seat must circulate, at his or her own expense, another proxy card to the shareholders. Yet even getting a list of shareholders in time for solicitation is virtually impossible since time-consuming litigation is usually required and entails even more expense.

Back when I was trying to secure a seat on the Sears board of directors—during a time when boneheaded management was driving share value into a canyon—I asked for a shareholder list and ended up being sued by the company, on the advice of Martin Lipton, who had been hired to thwart me, on the ingenious grounds that I was really trying to promote a book I had recently written. A founding partner of the powerhouse New York-based law firm Wachtell, Lipton, Rosen & Katz, Marty is sui generis, but such harassment is commonplace.

Given that the existing CEO and incumbent directors choose the individuals whose names will be on the proxy card and who will therefore be elected, it strains credulity to describe a director so created as independent of the management. A further stretch is required to accept that compensation

committees are anything like independent. In fact, a vast literature suggests just the opposite. Compensation committees are
peopled by and large—and quite intentionally—with those
directors most inclined to have a supportive view of CEO
compensation. Often committee members are being kept
on the board past normal retirement age exactly because they
are inclined to approve large packages for the man in charge.
Indeed, about the only way to get yourself thrown *off* a board
is to resist more money for the boss and to insist on greater
transparency in the payouts. Anything but that! As Warren
Buffett noted in his 2007 letter to Berkshire-Hathaway
shareholders, "Nobody invites me to be on compensation
committees."

Like the governance-rating agencies, the parallel subindustry of compensation consultants would have you believe
that theirs is an exacting science, full of hard bargaining
and subtle, finely honed calculations. Consider the following contractual clauses, describing John Snow's continuing
perquisites after his retirement as chairman and CEO of
CSX:

> For the remainder of his lifetime: country clubs,
> Greenbrier; executive physicals; financial and estate
> planning services; tax return preparation; and
> home security. Further, during the Term of this
> Agreement, the Executive shall continue to partici-
> pate in the Company's executive car allowance and
> charitable gift programs. Finally, the Executive shall
> be entitled to (i) unlimited use of Company aircraft
> or other comparable flight services during the
> Employment Period and the Chairmanship Period,
> if any, and (ii) thereafter, to reasonable and
> occasional use of Company aircraft or other com-
> parable flight services for the remainder of his life-
> time . . . [as well as provided] personal office and

secretarial support at a location of his choosing within the continental United States.

One can almost imagine Snow and CSX's compensation consultants locked in tense negotiation for hours, hammering out the ridiculous details of the future Treasury secretary's retirement—the Greenbrier or Augusta National? Commercial or private jets for those "comparable flight services"?—except that Snow's perquisites aren't fresh or new in the least. The preceding clauses are almost word for word the same as the similar perquisites worked out for Jack Welch at GE. It's not only nonsense; it's boilerplate nonsense. What's more, it's boilerplate nonsense negotiated by a compensation consultant who knew that neither he nor his firm would ever again work for John Snow, at CSX or wherever he might go next, or for any of Snow's CEO friends, at wherever they might be or go, if the terms were not ultimately pleasing to the man at the top.

On his 83rd birthday, Charles T. Munger, the Berkshire-Hathaway vice chairman and CEO of Wesco Financial, was asked by a reporter how CEO compensation had gotten so out of whack. Munger's answer, as recorded in the January 1, 2007, *Los Angeles Times:* "Some of the worst sinners are compensation consultants. I have always said that prostitution would be a step up for these people. 'Whose bread I eat, whose song I sing.'" That's harsh, but Charlie Munger has earned the right to be a little crotchety, and in this case, he also has the virtue of accuracy.

With the exception of such paragons as the late Marvin Bower, founder of McKinsey, I can think of virtually no examples of even the most principled leaders of professional service organizations who have imposed a culture of discouraging their clients' expectations and entitlements. That's not how you encourage return business, and it's certainly not the way things are done by 99 percent of compensation lawyers and consultants or by those agencies that, for a not nominal fee, provide ratings of corporate governance practices. The chimera is objectivity and the scientific method. The reality is self-perpetuating, self-protective, and rampant with conflicts of interest. The system is flawed up to its ears, and the more so because it pretends so earnestly to accuracy.

Ten years ago, Standard & Poor's developed a governance rating product based on all the "best practices" learned in its work with debt securities. Their professionals actually were given access to company personnel and records. Eventually, S&P was given permission by all the companies involved to publish the results, but the first client to authorize full disclosure was one who had received the highest possible ranking: Fannie Mae—the same Fannie Mae that was later found to have misstated earnings between 2001 and 2004 to hide a loss of more than $6 billion; the Fannie Mae that in the wake of the earnings scandal fired its finance chief Timothy Howard and independent auditor, KPMG; indeed the same Fannie Mae whose board simultaneously allowed CEO Franklin Raines to retire rather than be fired and lose a pension package that will pay Raines nearly $1.4 million a year for the rest of his life.

Fannie Mae's regulator, the Office of Federal Housing Enterprise Oversight (OFHEO), eventually issued a scathing 211-page report citing enough examples of insufficient controls and "pervasive and willful" accounting manipulations to launch an SEC inquiry and a criminal investigation by the Justice Department. But in some ways what is most interesting about the OFHEO report is the window it provides into the way even well-intentioned governance got thwarted at the top-rated lender. Here's what it had to say, in part:

> In 2003, the Compensation Committee sought to hire an executive compensation consultant who was to be accountable to the Committee rather than to management.

Nonetheless, Mr. Raines played a key role. In an undated letter from that year to Compensation Committee Chair Mulcahy, Kathy Gallo, Senior Vice President for Human Resources, wrote that the Fannie Mae management consultant on executive compensation, Alan Johnson Associates, recommended two firms that could serve as an independent Compensation Committee advisor: Fred Cook and Company and Brian Foley and Company. Ms. Gallo and Christine Wolf, Vice President for Compensation and Benefits, interviewed candidates from both firms. A subsequent September 2, 2003, letter to Ms. Mulcahy from Ms. Gallo, however, reflected the key role Mr. Raines played in Board decisions, even when it came to the actions of a Board committee on which he did not sit:

- "After our last conversation about an independent consultant to serve as the Committee's expert, I updated Frank on your readiness to explore the [Fred Cook] option. Frank was very much opposed to that idea because he has some significant concerns about both Fred's executive compensation philosophies and the way he sometimes advances his agenda on the topic.
- "Frank's concerns stem from observing Fred in a (distant) past interaction with the Fannie Mae board and more recently in the Business Roundtable meetings. Given that, Frank would strongly prefer that we not introduce anyone from Cook's organization into a compensation advisory role for Fannie Mae. I regret not spotting this issue before I proposed Brian to you."

Gallo subsequently recommended two additional candidates for consideration, both of whom presumably were acceptable to the CEO. One of them, Semler Brossy, was finally selected by the Compensation Committee to serve as Fannie Mae's independent consultant. "Management thus appears to have orchestrated the selection process to ensure that a consultant CEO Raines opposed did not receive the contract," the report concludes. This, too, is independence and governance in our times. Henry McKinnell must have been thrilled to have Raines serving on his board at Pfizer, just as Lee Raymond undoubtedly was pleased to have McKinnell among his directors.

Boards, compensation committees, and CEOs can be equally opaque when it comes to what should be the most transparent of facts: how much executives are paid. Much about compensation is required to be publicly disclosed—not just internal numbers but comparative data from other companies, times, and countries are readily available. In the whole field of corporate governance, no other category combines such a high level of transparency and numerical expression, and none, it seems, encourages greater obfuscation.

The May 2006 annual meeting of Home Depot was both a spectacle and a deeply depressing commentary on the state of governance in American corporations. Outside the Wilmington, Delaware, hotel where the meeting was held, a group of protestors, one dressed in a large chicken suit, gathered to protest the roughly $150 million paid to date to CEO Robert Nardelli even though Home Depot stock had declined in price during the nearly six years Nardelli had been at the helm. They were joined by a small group from People for the Ethical Treatment of Animals, demonstrating against the retail giant's sale of glue traps for mice, rats, and other pests.

Inside the meeting room, though, the varmints had scurried for the corners. On the stage, Nardelli sat almost alone, joined only by the company's corporate lawyer and a sign-language interpreter. His board of directors, the head of the board's various governance committees, and top management had all found pressing reasons not to attend. Just about their sole public comment on Nardelli's pay had come in a regulatory filing, where they maintained that it reflected "competitive levels of compensation for CEOs managing operations of similar size, complexity, and performance level" — this although Wal-Mart's CEO was earning less than half what Nardelli pulled down.

Faced with so little potential reward, only 50 or so shareholders or their representatives showed up for the presentation. One who did, Richard Ferlauto of the American Federation of State, County and Municipal Employees, which he said controls 4 percent of Home Depot's stock, tried to pick up on the avian theme from outside. The company's board were "chicken" for refusing to face the music. When he got to Nardelli's pay, Ferlauto switched metaphors, comparing it to the famous canary in a coal mine as a measure of both accountability and corporate governance. "Here at the Home Depot," he told the CEO, "I'm afraid that canary has died."

Nardelli sat stony-faced through Ferlauto's comments as he did through the others. His reply to each was a terse thank-you. In 30 minutes, the sole opportunity offered annually for Home Depot to meet its owners was history— over and done with, and all on the CEO's terms. Yet imagine how the scene might have gone if the protestors outside and if Ferlauto and others inside could have looked into a crystal ball and seen that, in addition to the $150 million-plus he had pocketed to date, Nardelli was within seven-and-a-half months of being awarded an additional $210 million in a severance package.

In fact, no one outside the golden circle of Home Depot's top management and directors had access to any of this information. Yes, shareholders knew that Nardelli was due an automatic $20 million cash severance. They knew that he would be automatically vested in a pension that was guaranteed at a minimum annual benefit of $2,250,000. But what would the lump sum cost be? How would it be reduced if Nardelli left before the normal retirement age of 62? If they read the fine print carefully, shareholders were aware that all his equity awards would vest immediately on severance, but how much were such awards worth in total? Values were indeed placed on these elements, but only after the fact. Before the fact, there was no way for shareholders to calculate the total cost of severance and thus no way to know if it would cost more to get rid of Nardelli than to keep him. How can shareholders even begin to exercise the most basic fiduciary responsibilities of ownership when such essential information is routinely denied them?

This is nuts, and it goes on ad infinitum and without apology. The final piece of Nardelli's golden parachute puzzle disclosed in January 2007 was "the payment of $18 million for other entitlements under his contract," to quote Home Depot. But $18 million for what? What were the entitlements? How had they been earned? To a man walking out the door with $210 million, a mere $18 million must be chump change, but to the average Home Depot shareholder, it's a pot of gold. Inquiries to the company led me nowhere.

Through his book, *Authentic Leadership*, in numerous speeches, and via the pulpit afforded him as a professor of management at Harvard Business School, Bill George, the former CEO and chairman at Medtronics, has become one of the foremost proponents of the need to bring basic ethical values back into the executive suite and the boardrooms of the United States' leading corporations. I heard him speak eloquently on these subjects at a forum sponsored by *Fortune* magazine in Aspen during the summer of 2003. Yet when I asked him afterward how much he had been paid as the Medtronics CEO, George refused to answer. Instead, he contented himself with saying, "You can't imagine the pressure my compensation committee put on me to accept more." I can understand his wanting to avoid my question, but to me, basic ethical values in the executive suite begin with being honest about what ought to be—but decidedly is not—a publicly available fact.

Four years later, during another Aspen conference, George approached me after one session and asked, "What can we do about executive compensation?" I replied, "Peer group leadership." His question was sincere: George is a fine person, and his conundrum with regard to executive compensation explains the scope of the problem. But my answer was equally sincere. Until enlightened CEOs finally say "Enough!" wanton greed will continue to drive the process.

I thought of Bill George's and my two exchanges when I read the Charlie Munger interview cited earlier. "It isn't that the CEOs are such terrible people," he said. "It's that the system, with its envy-driven compensation mania, has developed to a place where it brings out the absolute worst in good people."

I thought of Lou Gerstner, too. By all accounts, Gerstner is the "best of breed." From McKinsey through IBM, he has always gotten top marks. Gerstner is one of the few CEOs who can truly be said to have added value to their enterprise, and he was rewarded for it as he should have been. There was nothing chintzy about Gerstner's compensation at IBM, and yet even he couldn't stay away from the feeding frenzy. As he left IBM with his nest well feathered by a lavish retirement package, Gerstner accepted a further *douceur* of 125,000 shares, valued at around $13 million, simply as a kind of going-away present.

Though I've never considered him the best of the best, I thought of John Snow as well. Not only did his board forgive him a $10-million loan. Not only did it agree to those country-club memberships for life and those "comparable flight services." It also used a particularly odious tool known as a Supplemental Executive Retirement Plan (SERP) to credit Snow with 19 years of service he didn't perform and then allowed him to cash out his steroid-enriched pension at $33 million. Enough apparently is never enough.

The ultimate reality of American corporate governance is that CEOs have used their power, first, to pay themselves as much as possible; second, to obscure what they are legally required to disclose so as to blur objective scrutiny; third, to treat as a normal entitlement such steps as backdating options to enhance returns to which they were ostensibly entitled; and, fourth, to transfer as much of their real compensation to categories where disclosure was not strictly required, creating a treasure house of stealth compensation. This is an ugly picture, yet to ignore it is to fail to come to grips with the essential difficulty of accommodating a greed-based system with the well-being of society—the ultimate challenge for modern capitalism.

"Power tends to corrupt and absolute power corrupts absolutely." The Founding Fathers knew it as surely as Lord Acton. That is why they enshrined a system of checks and balances in the Constitution—so a despotic president or Congress or court could not seize power from its true owners, the American people. Although they have almost unimaginable economic clout, though they span the globe, employ tens of millions, and control vital natural resources, American corporations have no similar restraints. They cherry-pick which laws to obey, hide vital information deep in SEC filings, settle fortunes on their monarchs, and conspire with their supposed regulators to shut share-holders out of any meaningful ownership position. Corpor-ations hire legions of lawyers to circumvent statutes, pay sycophantic rating agencies to certify their open govern-ance, co-opt legislators, and seduce key elements of the media into believing that they are as dedicated to the rule of law as ever was Jefferson or Madison or Monroe. Corpor-ate oversight is not only a nullity. It is a sham.

In the early 1980s the federal government made an effort to cap what were then thought to be excessive executive salaries. The law denied tax deductibility for payments in excess of $1 million per year except to the extent they were based on performance criteria. And how did corporations respond? First, by ignoring the limit and paying the taxes, thus incurring extra cost for shareholders; and second by adopting compensation criteria that could easily be dis-torted and changed (Figure 5.1). So the story went before. So it went then. So it has gone ever since.

Full information about the compensation of the five top corporate officers has been mandated in a variety of forms for many years. There has never been any suggestion that the required information would describe only a limited portion of what the officers in fact receive. Yet when the SEC announced new disclosure policies to go into effect in 2007, they were greeted as a transforming departure from the past. They aren't. As with so much else in the corporate world, these new rules relating to compensation disclosure have been improved by ingenious lawyers into a refined minimalist compliance. Those of us who seek exact com-pensation information will still be confronted with see-mingly precise numbers that turn out to be uncorrelated with economic realities. What's more, noncompliance will remain a virtually risk-free response.

As a practical matter, what is the penalty for misstating an officer's compensation? Has there ever been an SEC

Year	Corporate Profits (%)	S&P (%)	Average CEO Pay (%)
1990	0.00	0.00	0.00
1991	0.00	4.51	25.00
1992	1.16	24.22	90.00
1993	9.30	33.21	90.00
1994	13.95	46.35	45.00
1995	25.58	42.95	90.00
1996	33.72	93.27	190.00
1997	38.37	138.90	290.00
1998	19.77	197.89	430.00
1999	19.77	288.85	520.00
2000	8.14	323.90	555.00
2001	-1.16	315.10	450.00
2002	11.63	243.44	270.00
2003	19.77	160.03	305.00
2004	33.72	243.72	380.00
2005	43.02	258.96	575.00
2006	60.47	288.99	635.00

- The Corporate Profit numbers come from the U.S. Department of Commerce Bureau of Economic Analysis.
- The S&P numbers come from Yahoo! Finance.
- The CEO Pay numbers come from TCL and are based on the *BusinessWeek* list.

- The chart above shows the cumulative percentage of change from 1990 through 2006.
- The Consumer Price Index numbers come from the U.S. Department of Labor Bureau of Labor Statistics.

Figure 5.1 Growth in CEO Compensation *vs.* Other Common Economic Measures

enforcement action? Can any investor prove that this caused damage? What even is the incentive for government to enforce these rules? With taxes, there exists at least the realistic prospect of penalties and prosecution in cases of negligently or intentionally misstated income. Not so with SEC disclosure forms. They are for the most part toothless wonders, another part of a tired dance meant to convince us that oversight exists when the opposite is far closer to the truth.

How anyone can still believe it is so, or even pretend to such belief, beggars imagination. Yet as recently as November 30, 2006, when the very establishmentarian Committee on Capital Market Regulation issued its Interim Report on how to keep U.S. capital markets globally competitive, committee members were still paying lip service to the idea that, where executive compensation was concerned, the times they were a'changing. Here is a sample from the report:

> An important debate over shareholder rights concerns the proper role of shareholders in the setting and review of executive compensation packages. Informing the public debate, there is a large and rapidly growing body of academic research exploring the subject.
>
> Before rendering any policy recommendations on the role of shareholder rights in the context of executive compensation, the Committee believes it is necessary to assess the impact of three important recent regulatory changes on executive compensation practices: (i) the SEC's sweeping new executive compensation disclosure requirements; (ii) new stock option expensing requirements; and (iii) compensation processing requirements. These new regulations, either individually or cumulatively, could well have an impact on executive compensation practices that should be

evaluated before policy recommendations can be crafted. In addition, the new SEC executive compensation disclosure requirements will provide a substantially more accurate picture of both the composition and size of executive compensation that will provide a firmer foundation for any policy recommendations in the area.

Baloney. The excess compensation of CEOs came about through a fundamental shift in attitudes both within and beyond the world of Big Business. A CEO was no longer simply a manager, the leader of a team of managers each of whom was effective at the level expected of them. Under the new dispensation, a CEO became the incarnation of charisma, without whom the company will collapse, value destroyed, and shareholders including widows and orphans left bereft. That's not the case within all boards and at all companies. Some CEOs are schmucks and are treated as such. Some are even abused by their boards and shareholders. Generalities are just that—general. But the larger the corporation, the greater its reach and heft, the more this shift in perception toward the philosopher-king CEO has settled in.

This perception is what justifies grotesque employment agreements. It props up a policy of paying enormous amounts of performance-unrelated compensation on being offered employment and while in the job. The shift in perception also underlies the remarkable arithmetic of instant vesting and the SERP-related habit of adding phantom years of service to enrich already Midas-like retirement packages. It even explains a pervasive dysfunctionality that allows principal corporate officers to control the circumstances under which their behavior is monitored and by which they are paid and let go. The Business Roundtable and CEOs generally cite their high turnover rate as part of the market that sets executive pay, but the CEOs themselves have negotiated contracts that make it more valuable for them to be fired than to continue working. So perverse is the current system and so acquiescent are those on the board who should be monitoring such things that it is often in the interest of CEOs to trigger their firing provisions rather than to do the job in such a way as to assure their continued employment. How nuts is that? And the sad fact is that there is almost no hope that this situation will be altered or even challenged by boards of directors who have proven themselves willing servants of a colossal fraud. As the noted governance expert Nell Minow put it: "If the board can't get executive compensation right, it's been shown it won't get anything else right either."

There is a model for where the corpocracy is taking us. It is to be found in a country where the conversion from state to private ownership has resulted in the accumulation of massive shares of the industry and national wealth by a small class of citizens. In this country, the corporate sector helped to elect a president by funding a vast advertising campaign. Later, when a new president was elected, he struck a deal with the corporate warlords. He wouldn't disturb their ownership arrangements or attempt to impose any sort of governance so long as they kept out of politics. When an oil magnate, one of the wealthiest industrialists in the country, threatened to break the pact and began calling for greater financial transparency, equal footing for all shareholders, and a strong corporate governance charter, the government acted decisively to imprison him under severe conditions and to dismember his business. Meanwhile, the nation's other major industrialists are grabbing all the money they can. As has been the pattern in the United States, these massive transfers of wealth are in accord with what is considered to be lawful.

The nation, no surprise, is Russia, where the rapacious CEOs are known as *oligarchs* and don't even pretend to a social conscience or any obligation to the public good. That might be more honest than the high-brow nonsense spouted by many of our own philosopher-king industrialists, but is it really where the American corporation wants to be heading?

Chapter Six

HOUSE TAKE

On Friday May 10, 1901, a three-story house at 10 Broad Street in lower Manhattan was demolished and replaced by a neoclassical building that featured one of the largest interior spaces in the whole expansive city: the new trading floor of the rapidly growing New York Stock Exchange (NYSE).

Broad Street had long been a trading center—in the 1600s, when the street was still a canal, Native Americans canoed in with vegetables—but as the nineteenth century ended, the Exchange was morphing into a marketplace the likes of which no one had seen. By 1901, the NYSE's trading volume had increased tremendously, growing sixfold in the previous five years. Now far and away the dominant national exchange, the NYSE and its management wanted a building that suggested institutional trust and solidity in the midst of the sometimes roller-coaster fortune rides on the trading floor. The façade of the new building—with a marble sculpture in the pediment titled "Integrity Protecting the Works of Man"—symbolized the honesty and reliability that the NYSE hoped would be associated with the Exchange for many years to come. In part because of its success in maintaining this reputation, the Exchange—also known as the "Big Board"—today ranks as the largest stock exchange in the world by dollar volume. With more than $17 trillion in market value of listed securities, the NYSE has even moved aggressively into European markets in recent years.

As it has grown in power and prestige, the Big Board has become both a symbol of national strength and a target for the enemies of capitalism and the United States. About noon on September 16, 1920, just around the corner from the NYSE, a horse-drawn cart filled with dynamite exploded in front of the offices of J. P. Morgan, ripping the façade off the building, decapitating an innocent passerby, killing another 29 people, and injuring a hundred. Thought to be the work of anarchists although no arrests were ever made, the attack caused the Exchange to close for the first time in the face of violence. When Wall Street went back to work the next day, a crowd said to number in the thousands stood in front of the Morgan headquarters singing "America the Beautiful." In case the point was lost, newspapers reported the next day that the defiant, patriotic financial workers were "determined to show the world that business will proceed as usual despite bombs."

Exactly 81 years later, on September 17, 2001, Wall Street repeated the scene, this time in the wake of far greater violence. With the dust still settling from the destruction of the World Trade Center, Big Board CEO Richard Grasso—flanked by senators, firemen, and policemen— reopened the NYSE once again. Pointing to the Exchange as emblematic of the nation's resilience, Grasso told the crowd assembled on the floor and a global television audience: "Today, America goes back to business, and we do it as a signal to those criminals who inflicted this heinous crime on America and Americans that they have lost."

After two minutes of silence, the market resumed trading and promptly plunged 600 points as traders rushed to fill sell orders that had built up over the past six days. There was no widespread panic, though. Indeed, within months the market had recovered and resumed its upward climb. All that is a story much told and celebrated. Far less mentioned is the cost of much of the market's recent success.

Throughout the bulk of its history, the NYSE had used its privileged position in American financial markets to enforce basic principles of corporate governance. During the nineteenth and early twentieth centuries, the exchange threatened to delist companies that didn't provide information to shareholders. It wasn't an idle threat: The NYSE was the *Good Housekeeping* Seal of Approval, something everyone could count on.

Today, although it remains a prestigious and wealthy club, the Big Board has all but abandoned its role as a guardian of corporate governance and stockholder trust along with its insistence on institutional accountability. Swept up by the rising prestige and income of financial sector workers and in some critical ways responsible for both, the Exchange has taken on the characteristics and mindset of some of the most aggressive corporations whose shares it trades.

Oddly, it took the worst sell-off in history to produce the greatest reforms. On October 24, 1929, one of the sharpest market upswings in history—a two-year spike that saw the Dow Jones Industrial Average (DJIA) soar by nearly 250 percent—came to a near-cataclysmic end. The sell-offs that began that Black Thursday didn't bottom out until July 1932 when the DJIA closed nearly 89 percent off its September 1929 peak. By then, there was no denying that the boom that had turned into such a bust had been fed not just by the usual irrational exuberance of investors but also by mismanagement, deception, and outright fraud.

Swept into the presidency in 1932 with a mandate for regulation of the financial markets, Franklin Roosevelt and his advisors moved quickly to create both a legal framework for trading public shares and a new quasi-juridical agency for regulating the entire industry. Two New Deal programs in particular—the U.S. Securities Act of 1933 and the U.S. Securities Exchange Act of 1934—represented both a sweeping transformation of the rules by which shares could be bought and sold, and an ambitious attempt to set up a process of corporate accountability, an impartial set of rules that would preserve the widest possible latitude for shareholders to protect their financial interests.

In searching for a reliable and familiar model for this goal, Congress borrowed from the United States' political traditions: three distinct branches, each of which was empowered to check the abuses of the other. In this alignment, shareholders were seen as voters, boards of directors as elected representatives, the CEO as a president, proxy solicitations as election campaigns, and corporate charters and bylaws as constitutions and amendments. Just as political democracy acted to guarantee the legitimacy of government and public power, so corporate democracy would control and legitimate the otherwise uncontrollable growth and abuse of power and money in the hands of private individuals.

Underpinning this corporate democracy was the principle of one share, one vote. Because voting is meaningful only when information about the company is widely available to shareholders, the 1933 Act set out rigorous and complete standards of disclosure, sufficient for prudent investors to sniff out fraud and corruption. As one of the Securities and Exchange Commission's greatest scholars, Louis Loss, wrote, "The Act does not prevent a person from making a fool of himself; it prevents someone else from making a fool out of him." The 1934 Act went further still; it regulated the crucial area of proxy solicitation and voting, the means by which shareholders exercised oversight of management.

Roosevelt subsequently signed other legislation, including the Public Utility Holding Company Act of 1935 and the

Investment Company Act of 1940 that further upheld the one-share, one-vote principle by prohibiting multiple classes of common stock. In the 1934 Securities Exchange Act, Congress also brought the previously independent stock exchanges, and therefore all publicly quoted companies, under the aegis of the new Securities and Exchange Commission, an agency created to administer the entire framework of corporate democracy.

Although the nation was still struggling its way through the Great Depression, Congress and the president between them had erected an entire new system of corporate accountability, a framework explicitly based on the assumption that American shareholders were proprietary owners of the businesses they had invested in, both willing and able to hold managers responsible for their actions. In theory, this was the beginning of the Golden Age of shareholder democracy. In practice, multiple forces would soon rise up to undermine that democracy before it could ever take root.

First among the forces was the atomization of corporate ownership. The end of the robber baron era and the dispersion of their vertical trusts had combined with the rapid increase in disposable wealth before World War I and the Wall Street boom of the late 1920s to draw Americans into the stock market in record numbers. By the end of the next sustained bull market—the early 1950s, when the Dow Jones finally reached and passed its 1929 high—every publicly traded major corporation had tens of thousands, even millions of owners. That was the good news: The populace was sharing in the growth of corporate wealth as never before. The downside of this rush to participation was that almost no single owner possessed a stake large enough to justify the very expensive and time-consuming process of trying to unseat incompetent management when share value lagged. Instead, most shareholders adopted what became known as the "Wall Street Rule": If you disagree with management, hold your nose and sell your stock.

That is the essence of rational behavior, but it, too, had a downside. Over time, shareholders came to treat their stocks not as property that they could work to improve but as betting slips: Putting money on General Motors was like risking it on a horse or dog. The initial bet required one's best judgment of form and conditions, but after that there was little anyone, least of all the bettor, could do to alter performance. Instead of any feeling of proprietary involvement with the companies that were collectively their personal property, shareholders became intentionally inactive. Congress, it turned out, had given shareholders elaborate means to hold managers accountable just as shareholders were beginning to lose any interest in or motive for doing so.

Nonetheless, the NYSE remained a mostly useful ally of shareholders well into the 1950s. Famously, the Exchange had nudged the SEC into inventing the authority to require audits of listed companies by independent auditors, a practice essential to any semblance of honest bookkeeping. The Exchange had also generally enforced the one-share, one-vote rule since the 1920s—before it was legislated—by refusing to list any companies that offered stock with differing voting rights. (Imagine a democracy that granted 100 votes to those with a net worth in excess of $10 million, 50 votes to those with $5 to $10 million, and so on down to a single vote to those with zero or negative assets.) That a purchaser of shares on the Exchange should have the same voting rights as all other shareholders was one of the enabling myths of people's capitalism. Not for Americans the European practice of insiders with special voting privileges.

The Exchange's upholding of the one-share, one-vote principle was not merely an ethical stand; the NYSE had a long-term interest in maintaining the faith of investors in an honest, straightforward share-trading system. However, the Exchange also had an interest in new listings, particularly plum ones, and when these two motivations clashed, the Big Board's managers could not ignore their commercial leanings.

In 1956, the Ford family decided to take one of the largest American companies public with two classes of stock—a Class A stock for the general public and a Class B stock with superweighted voting privileges for Henry Ford's heirs. Faced with a choice between principles and pragmatism, the NYSE abandoned its iron-clad allegiance to one share, one vote, and shareholder democracy began to crumble for good. Today, the Ford family owns about a 4 percent equity in the company that bears its name but controls 40 percent of the voting rights, which it almost always exercises as a bloc, virtually guaranteeing that even a bumbling CEO like Bill Ford will never be replaced so long as he bears the family DNA.

Yet another force undermining shareholder democracy was let loose on May Day 1975 when Wall Street nervously stepped into an uncertain future. This was the "last day of the club"—the day when fixed-commission trading stopped on the New York Stock Exchange. Heretofore, brokers had operated within a cozy, virtually monopolistic system that required, and attracted, a limited degree of competence. Now, they could negotiate commission rates, a possibility for almost limitless riches that seems to have excited few of the brokers affected. Instead, as Robert J. Cole reported in the May 2, 1975, *New York Times*, many spent the day sweating out the coming rates showdown with their biggest clients. "Stockbrokers watched each other more closely than ever, looking for signs of what might be happening," Cole wrote. "They checked again and again with their big clients—banks, pension funds, insurance companies and mutual funds—but often got little more than indications they would be hard bargainers."

It wasn't long, however, before the smartest brokers and brokerage houses realized that what the NYSE had really done on May 1, 1975, was to remove the last feudal obstacles to full commercial expression of the world's premier trading market. When DLJ (the investment bank of Donaldson, Lufkin, and Jenrette) put itself up for public offering so that the partners could get their money out, the nature of such institutions changed utterly. No longer would people get paid for just showing up. They had to sell; they had to move things. The Great Hustle was on.

The results have been both explosive and revolutionary. Five years after the club was closed down, the financial-markets industry was worth about $22 billion compared with manufacturing's $78 billion. Just 10 years later, the financial markets' collective worth had soared to about $73 billion, fast closing in on manufacturing's $113 billion. By 2004, finance not only had overtaken manufacturing but, at $218 billion, was worth more than twice manufacturing's shrinking $105 billion.

Today, the financial sector, not manufacturing, not information, not high-tech or high science is the driving force of the American economy for one extremely simple reason: The largest and most profitable industry in the United States, indeed the most profitable the world has ever seen, is the trading and management of pieces of paper—or digital computer blips—evidencing borrowing and ownership. What matters now is not making and selling things. That's Old World. What really matters in today's world is ownership of the companies that do such things, the creation of different kinds of instruments representing an infinite variety of risks and rewards, and the removal of all friction so that this vast slicing and dicing can go on as instantaneously and as unimpeded as humanly and electron-ically possible—including the friction inherent in the belief that ownership of an entity might entail any sort of obli-gation to it.

For the most part, this orgy of unfettered buying and selling is legitimate and even smart. By playing all available angles, investors who truly understand what's happening can all but provide virtual protection for themselves on the downside while reaping huge gains on the upside. But the overall effect has been to turn the NYSE into a gigantic, round-the-clock casino that runs the biggest game the world has ever seen. The handle is huge—the market value of the listed companies multiplied by the infinite iterations through which it is traded—as is the house take, the vigorish, the skim on the balance. Think of the exchange as Vegas East, or Atlantic City North, or as the American Monte Carlo because that is basically exactly how it makes its money.

Inevitably, this vast financial success has presaged a shift in national values. Today, American priorities—informed and shaped by the language of economics—are generally to subordinate all other considerations in assuring the unim-peded workings of the financial markets. Indeed, the mar-ket has become the medium through which all worthwhile objectives are to be achieved. Market values have become national values. Market index averages are a national obses-sion. Market goals have become political ones as well, especially a global expansion of American interests that is far more extensive and profitable than even in the great age of traditional industrial commerce.

Even when the market is manifestly corrupted by inadequate and contrived flows of information, American policy—some-times styled neoliberalism—is based on the conviction that the expansion of free markets will maximize socioeconomic wealth. The corollary is that whatever impedes the smooth flow of financial markets is to be avoided at all costs, including maybe most especially the messy entanglements of share-holder democracy. Beneficial owners, so the reasoning goes, are ultimately a pain in the neck.

Not surprisingly and again inevitably, this shift in the importance of markets and the massive fees commanded by brokers have attracted many of the nation's smartest college graduates to the financial profession. Looking back on trends of recent decades, former Harvard President Derek Bok recently commented, "Not only did the numbers of young people entering schools of law and business double and treble; their intellectual level rose significantly. In 1950, law and MBA students were only of average ability; their test scores were far below those of classmates in medical schools, engineering or graduate (PhD) studies. By 1990, the situation had changed; the quality of students seeking admission to schools of law and business now rivaled that of applicants to any other graduate or professional school."

A half century ago, the cream of the college crop was likely to end up in the CIA if they had Yale credentials, or on something like Bob McNamara's Falcon team at Ford. By the late-1980s and certainly by the early 1990s, the best and the brightest had begun flocking to investment banking. That is where the prestige was, where the allure pointed, and where the smell of money was most unmistakable. And no place by then was more steeped in all three characteristics than Goldman Sachs, one reason that it is known to insiders simply as "The Firm."

In fact, Goldman Sachs has always been ahead of the game. Headquartered two blocks down Broad Street from the Exchange, where it has been a member since 1896, The Firm was one of the nineteenth-century pioneers in issuing commercial paper. Later it moved on to initial public offerings of many large stocks, including Sears Roebuck in 1906. In the early twentieth century, The Firm also became one of the first finance companies to recruit recent MBA degrees from top business schools, even when the "top" wasn't very high.

Goldman Sachs' reputation suffered a severe setback in the fall of 1929 when its own start-up, Goldman Sachs Trading (GST), turned out to be mostly a Ponzi scheme. Three years later, GST stock, which had been issued to some 40,000 investors for $104 a share, was trading for less than $2 a share. By the early 1970s, however, The Firm had long since crawled out of its hole and was already beginning to assemble the all-star cast that would help it ride the coming boom.

Goldman Sachs alumni include current Treasury Secretary Henry Paulson; Robert Rubin, who held the same post in the Clinton administration; former U.S. Senator and now New Jersey Governor Jon Corzine; former Deputy Secretary of State John Whitehead; White House Chief of Staff Josh Bolten; even the raving clown prince of stock pickers, Jim Cramer, host of CNBC's *Mad Money*. Goldman Sachs remains today a premier destination for newly minted MBAs anxious to reach for the stars, and with good reason. In mid-December 2006, The Firm announced that it had earned more than $9.3 billion for the year on revenues of $37.7 billion and was setting aside $16.5 billion for salaries, bonuses, and benefits—or $622,000 an employee, including secretaries and mail clerks.

In the *Star Wars* mythology that built up around Wall Street in the 1970s and 1980s, Goldman Sachs was home to the Jedi battling the dark force of Darth Vader, conveniently played by Michael Milken and other junk-bond artists and so-called corporate raiders. The Firm was the first brokerage house to employ the "White Knight" strategy, back in 1974 while attempting to defend Electric Storage Battery against a hostile takeover bid from International Nickel and Goldman Sachs's rival Morgan Stanley. (In the White Knight gambit, a hostile takeover bid is thwarted when a company friendly to the target steps up with an offer the board can accept.)

Top management increasingly turned to Goldman Sachs as more and more barbarians began to storm the gates. For The Firm and its partners, that was money in the bank, huge piles of it. For the raiders, it was mostly bad news. (It's an intriguing sidelight of modern business-related jurisprudence that, until Enron, jail time was meted out almost exclusively to raiders such as Milken who challenged entrenched power. CEOs, it seems, could level small towns through their negligence and walk away scot-free.) In between these warring parties stood the shareholders, and the shareholders and any semblance of shareholder democracy mostly got trampled in the charges and counter-charges.

To protect against the legitimate efforts of raiders to use their stock-ownership positions to institute proxy fights to clear out deadwood directors and management—and ultimately underperforming assets—from frequently floundering companies, the regulators refused to clarify and simplify proxy requirements to the point where beneficial owners were excluded for practical purposes from any say in company affairs.

No *quo* was more meaningful than the status quo, and thanks to regulatory indifference, no charade became more complete than a proxy-fight charade. The artifice is that reforms have eased the proxy process. The continuing reality is that company bylaws require that proposals be submitted months ahead of the annual meeting so that the corporate lawyers will have time to convince the SEC's censorship division to disallow any proposals management finds objectionable. Notice that a proposal has been disallowed almost never arrives until days before the proxy statement is in the mail, and there is virtually no effective appeal in such cases to the courts or to the full SEC commission. By then, the train has left the station and won't stop until it arrives at an annual corporate convocation that is about as rigged and foreordained as any mockery of democracy could be.

Similarly, to nip the problem at the root, regulators turned an increasingly blind eye to that old bane of shareholder democracy and corporate accountability: shares segregated by voting right. One likes to think that in 1956, NYSE managers wrestled mightily with whether to list Ford and its A- and B-class stocks before finally raising their skirts. Almost three decades later, in 1984, the Big Board never blinked when General Motors issued a second tier of stock as part of its purchase of Ross Perot's Electronic Data Systems. By then, what was good for financial markets was good for America.

Two years later, in 1986, all these disparate forces finally came to a head. To stay competitive with other exchanges that had stopped paying even lip service to shareholder democracy, the NYSE put forward a proposal to drop its one-share, one-vote rule altogether. Simultaneously, the powerful, informed, and active shareholder that the original 1930s New Deal legislation envisioned was coming into its majority in the form of private pension funds.

Pension funds predate the 1974 passage of the Employee Retirement Income Security Act, but ERISA gave them a fresh track to run on and unambiguous instructions of how to behave. By 1986, pension funds and mutual funds, which were first organized under the 1940 Act, collectively held one third of American publicly traded stocks; by 2000, they owned more than 60 percent. About half of that is in pension funds, which like mutual funds have seen explosive growth over the past several decades. One pension fund alone—the California Public Employees' Retirement System

(CalPERS)—has $218 billion in assets and serves one million members.

Although these massive pension funds have managers, the ERISA statute requires that each trustee "discharge his duties . . . solely in the interest of the participants and beneficiaries and for the exclusive purpose of providing benefits to participants and their beneficiaries." The manager must also act "with the care, skill, prudence and diligence" that a prudent man of similar expertise and experience would use in similar circumstances. Put simply, pension fund trustees and managers have a legal obligation to act as owners, an obligation that is public, explicit, and contained in a single federal statute that preempts the uncertainties and inconsistencies of state law. They also have goals—in the form of retirement payouts to their members—that are well-defined, predictable through actuarial projections, and long-term. As Peter Drucker has written, "The only performance that counts in the pension fund is performance over the long run, since the obligations extend over 25 years or longer."

Pension funds as active investors are still coming into their political maturity and too often getting the back of the hand from regal CEOs when they try to exercise their obligations at annual shareholder meetings. But it is not a great stretch to imagine a time when the funds might develop both the will to demand attention and the muscle to compel it. Take a proxy solicitation to remove the directors of a large but poorly performing company. Pension funds are almost certain to own a collective stake in the company large enough to justify soliciting votes. They have the necessary financial and legal expertise to understand the costs, benefits, and means of doing so. They face significant costs if they choose to sell their stock and reinvest the cash elsewhere, and they have a clear legal liability if they fail to act in the beneficiaries' best interests.

Whether soliciting proxies or simply making known their continuing concerns, pension funds would be acting rationally and in their own best interests—precisely in accord with the model of the energetic and informed shareholder-owners that Congress anticipated in the mid-1930s.

Maybe because regulators were looking into that same crystal ball and seeing the "inefficiencies" of a true shareholder democracy—or because the Business Roundtable had already seen the future and didn't want it, or the NYSE was feeling AMEX (American Stock Exchange) and Nasdaq breathing down its neck—the SEC held hearings on December 16–17, 1986, to initiate the process of eliminating the one-share, one-vote rule. I was allowed to speak and urged the commission against doing away with what is really the core of corporate governance.

"If the SEC now drops the one-share, one-vote rule," I said, "it will be directly repudiating both the intent and the continuing policies of a 50-year-old commitment to corporate democracy." I also argued that, as a practical matter, dropping the rule will end the need for management to be responsible for its actions to corporate shareholders and pointed out the irony that the hearings were being held precisely as the active, participatory shareholder was emerging. Finally, I reminded the commission of the terminal nature of pulling this requirement on businesses listed with the Exchange: "After a certain number of companies have recapitalized [to create dual-voting rights], it is certain to prove politically and economically impossible for the NYSE to reverse its policy once again."

I went on to suggest a worst-case scenario—the eventual rot in capitalism that disenfranchising shareholders could create. As the owners lose even the theoretical ability to control their corporations or hold their managers to account, those corporations will cease to pay attention even to the need to maximize profits. Business will become bloated and inefficient, performance will drop, and the unchecked manager's focus will shift to self-enrichment. Further, once it becomes readily apparent that the mechanisms of corporate control are illusory—that illegitimate private power has gone unchecked for too long—then the rationale for state and federal governments not intervening in the private sphere will disappear. Governmental interference and regulation will be seen as the natural alternative, with predictably disastrous results. In the rush to check its excesses, American corporate capitalism will come to resemble European corporate socialism.

I can't swear to the effectiveness of my dark testimony, but I like to think it had an effect because on July 7, 1988, the SEC passed a compromise rule change by a vote of 4 to 1, requiring the exchanges to bar the listing of any corporation that acted to reduce the voting rights of any class of shareholders. Even this modest rule change, however, drew the furious attention of the Business Roundtable, which immediately launched litigation contending that the SEC had overstepped its authority by meddling in corporate governance matters traditionally left to the states. Two years later, on June 12, 1990, the DC federal appeals court essentially agreed, striking down the compromise rule harshly and unanimously.

"In 1934," the court wrote, "Congress acted on the premise that shareholder voting could work, so long as investors secured enough information and perhaps, the benefit of other procedural protections. It did not seek to regulate the stockholders' choices. If the Commission believes that premise misguided, it must turn to Congress. With its step beyond control of the voting procedure and into the distribution of voting power, the Commission would assume an authority that the Exchange Act's proponents disclaimed any intent to grant."

Although the appeals court had ruled that the SEC couldn't make the exchanges enforce a one-share, one-vote rule, the exchanges themselves weren't ready to abandon the principle entirely. For the BRT and its allies, that might have been a serious problem since one-share one-vote in theory facilitates hostile takeovers, but by then, Justice Powell's decision a year earlier in *CTS Corporation v. Dynamics Corp of America* had so chilled the possibilities of a takeover and so severely circumscribed the theoretical involvement of pension funds in any such action that BRT didn't feel the need to pursue additional protection in Congress. For those states that might choose to challenge the Roundtable and CEO absolutism, BRT had a simple solution readily at hand. As Marty Lipton, the best corporate lawyer in the nation, indelicately put it after a Delaware court had uncharacteristically found directors liable for negligence, "It may be that I will have to advise my clients to incorporate elsewhere."

That's pretty much where responsibility for the governance of American corporations sits today: uneasily split between direct federal involvement in such proxy-related matters as shareholder communications and applicable state law. Meanwhile, the NYSE, which seems incapable any longer of recognizing its own self-interest in promoting shareholder democracy, has been exuding an almost Bourbon flavor of imperial prosperity in recent years. And why not? The Big Board sits at the center of such limitless financial prosperity that none of its principals has the time or patience to even understand how much the CEO is paying himself.

Dick Grasso's $188-million pay package was roundly criticized as being wildly excessive when it was first revealed in 2004. But what was far more troubling was that such a gargantuan sum was so much in the spirit of the companies that Grasso, as the Big Board's CEO, was charged with overseeing. Indeed, as James Surowiecki pointed out in the January 22, 2007, *New Yorker*, the head of the compensation committee that approved Grasso's golden pay, Kenneth Langone, had earlier engineered Bob Nardelli's hiring at Home Depot, where he also served on the board. This is a man worth knowing. Nor, one should add, was the exorbitant pay package the first time Grasso had been richly rewarded by his board. For getting the market back to business on September 17, 2001, only six days after Armageddon, the exchange CEO was rewarded with a one-time bonus of $10 million. That might seem to be the job he was hired to do, but just doing the job in this market is never enough reward.

The joy ride, though, is coming to an end. The Big Board's impressive edifice on Broad Street is listed in the National Register of Historic Places, but its functions can largely be performed electronically, while its principal owners have operations all around the world and limited commitment to focusing operations in New York. Not only does the Exchange face mounting competition at home and abroad; new technologies are increasingly calling into question whether its cost structure can be justified. What's more, NYSE's major customers—the great mutual funds like Fidelity with over $1 trillion under management—are ready and able to create markets for their own use. Ironically, abandoning meaningful listing requirements and shying away from a leadership role in corporate governance means that the Exchange has squarely bet its commercial survival on the brutal game of economic competition. And others can play that game just as well, and just as dirty, as the NYSE can.

For all its flaws, the November 30, 2006, "Interim Report of the Committee on Capital Markets Regulation" seems to recognize as much. "Without adequate shareholder rights that provide accountability of directors and managements to shareholders, rational investors will reduce the price at which they are willing to purchase shares," the report's authors wrote, "Firms, therefore, would have an incentive either not to enter the U.S. public markets in the first place or to exit them in response to inadequate legal protection of shareholder rights.'' In other words, undercutting shareholders' rights—measures often taken in the name of economic competition—has now gone so far that U.S. markets may no longer be enticing for investors.

That's either a death knell for the stock exchanges, or the beginning of wisdom.

Chapter Seven

EFFICIENCIES "R" US

The assault on shareholder rights is only one of many consequences of the rise of corporate hegemony, and in some ways not the worst among them. In the name of maximizing profit and efficiency—and in the service of a new econocentric view of the obligation of employer to employee and government to the governed—pension systems are trampled, lifetime employment becomes a fast-dimming memory, and responsibilities once thought the prerogative of the state end up being privatized left and right.

Venerable community structures such as mutual insurance companies and savings and loans institutions were equally swept away through privatization, not to the benefit of the community certainly or to the policy or account holders but largely to provide the equity that would enrich chief executives who once had considered a large office and the admiration of their neighbors sufficient reward. The latter no longer mattered because the language of modern economics has no place for immeasurable qualities such as community well-being and fraternal strength.

The body politic suffered, too. Just as shareholder-owners retreated from corporate governance in the face of massive resistance to their participation, so voter-owners have retreated from participation in a political government that seems determined to rid itself of all duty to the general populace. Fringes from the left and right own the nominating process. The percentage of eligible voters who actually cast ballots sinks lower with each new election, or almost so. And everyone in the know pretends to wonder why. It's an amazement the pols and pundits can even keep a straight face when they talk about it.

At heart, all these tactical victories in the triumph of economics represent a transfer of wealth from one group to another: from government to private corporations, from pensioners to corporations and to their principal executives, from beneficiaries of pension and mutual-fund arrangements to service providers to those trusts.

Each of these transfers, in turn, is justified by the primacy of economic considerations. Public services are deemed a matter of cost-effectiveness. Income protection for aged workers is a sea anchor on the bottom line. At universities with multibillion-dollar endowments, adjunct-professor labor is exploited to avoid encumbering the health-plan rolls or incurring retirement obligations. Pension plans are "set free" to offer a panoply of services and financial instruments with the promise that a cafeteria approach is always best but with the underlying (and unstated) reality that "churning" the vast funds for which the pensions bear fiduciary responsibility will throw off huge fees that inevitably embed conflicts of interests between pensioners and mutual fund holders and their managers.

There was a reason the Bank of New York paid $16.5 billion to buy Mellon Bank in 2006, and it wasn't that Mellon ran the best bank in history, or even east of the Mississippi. The reason, simply put, was that Mellon was the trustee of valuable fiduciary relationships and that roiling up those relationships was certain to produce extraordinary wealth for those who did the stirring. Far less certain was whether the stirring would enrich those who had entrusted Mellon Bank with their economic futures, but that really has been the history of the past 35 years: the enrichment of intermediaries, of whom money managers are only the most conspicuous, and the impoverishment of beneficiaries.

Those who "make" things are fast disappearing. Since George W. Bush took office in January 2001, an astounding one in five U.S. manufacturing jobs has simply vanished— set sail and gone overseas, or across the border into Mexico. The language and mindset of economics as well as the politicians of both parties who front for economics tell us this is good, a necessary sop to the realities of a global and interrelated marketplace. Perhaps so—that's the subject of another book. But who all this is most good for in the short term are the churners, the money managers, the CEOs, the owners and principal executives of the businesses and financial service outfits that have been decoupled and set free to compete on what the corporate propagandists assure us is a newly leveled field. Here's the truth: It isn't. This rising tide isn't lifting all ships equally or semiequally or even fractionally equally. The great preponderance of wealth generated in recent years has gone to those who have devoted themselves to numerically expressed performance, to the liquidity of assets, and to a short-term perspective, which is why the richest Americans by far are increasingly hedge-fund and private-equity principals. That's where the churn washes ashore.

In its October 9, 2006, annual feature on the "Forbes 400," the self-proclaimed "Capitalist Tool" magazine listed what it called the "Cash Kings," more than 80 American billionaires with the power to move markets and make or break a business. The leveraged-buyout mogul Carl Icahn led the pack with a personal fortune that *Forbes* estimated to be nearly $10 billion, but if Icahn was the greatest in degree, he was not much different from the average in kind. Just about no one on the list had ever made anything tangible, or perhaps ever wanted to. Almost to a person, their vast fortunes had been garnered by moving money around—by manipulating debt, buying and flipping companies, and reaping management fees for their services. This is what it means to be "competitive" in the United States in the opening decade of the twenty-first century.

No institution has been more seduced by the primacy of money and the imperative of economic considerations than the largest institution of all: the U.S. government. Within living memory of many of us, the struggle over policy involved a Babel of tongues: history, ethics, politics, and law foremost among them. Legislation and regulation were expected to reflect tradition, a sense of fairness and legitimacy, a respect for property rights, and the abiding American commitment to egalitarianism. Over the past two to three decades, those debates have been superseded by the consideration of costs and benefits, which, conveniently, can be quantified and expressed numerically and thus rendered easily into the language of economics, the new *lingua franca* of politics.

Against this backdrop, the increasing power of large corporations has fueled a rush to privatize a wide spectrum of what were previously considered public services, even public responsibilities. To achieve "market efficiencies," basic oversight functions of public funds are abandoned to the very people receiving the money. In one highly publicized case, the U.S. Coast Guard's "Deepwater" program to modernize its aging fleet, two defense contractors—Lockheed Martin and Northrop Grumman—received wide latitude to police their own performance because the Coast Guard lacked the resources to monitor progress on its own. The results have been predictable as they almost always are when the fox gets inside the henhouse. Vessel after vessel turned out by the contracting team has been declared unseaworthy, including the crown in the jewel, the 418-foot cutter "National Security," which might never spend a day at sea unless serious design flaws can be overcome.

During the first six years of the George W. Bush presidency, the top 20 contractors providing services to the federal government nearly doubled their expenditures for lobbying, to more than $80 million. Meanwhile, the Bush administration—determined to privatize government services and faced with multiple crises, from Hurricane Katrina to 9/11 and Iraq—nearly doubled the value of federal contracts awarded to the private sector, to $400 billion, while simultaneously reducing the percentage of those contracts subject to full and open competition from 80 percent to under 50 percent, according to figures collected by the *New York Times*. The ongoing misery to be found in New Orleans, in Baghdad, and elsewhere in Iraq testifies to just how well the primacy of economics has served the public interest. This is what happens when efficiency becomes the end. Meanwhile, those same market efficiencies have turned Washington, in the person of Uncle Sam, into the largest customer in the world and the lawyers and lobbyists who represent corporate interests in the nation's capital into some of the United States' best-paid salespeople.

On Wall Street, pressure from corporations to circumvent the one-share one-vote rule and protect themselves from takeovers legitimatized multiple classes of stock. In Washington and in state capitals around the nation, pressure to toe the line on cost-benefit considerations has created an analogous assortment of multitier public services. To avoid the supposed economic inefficiencies and cost drags of universal health care, the United States has a three-tier system that ranges from Medicaid for the impoverished elderly, Medicare for those who quality for Social Security, and a hodgepodge of privately administered and highly profitable plans offered by mostly corporate HMOs, or health maintenance organizations. A fourth tier amounting to some 47 million Americans, including as many as 11 million children, goes uninsured, forced to rely mostly on free clinics and crumbling publicly supported hospitals, while private hospitals thrive. In another era, the health disenfranchisement of so many among us, especially the young, would have at least formed the basis for a vigorous public debate. In our own time, it is enough to say that the 47 million uninsured simply don't fit on a spreadsheet.

Roads, too, would seem to be a fundamental obligation of government, for travel and commerce, to accommodate the spread of cities and open up new areas for development. Begun as a defense measure under Dwight Eisenhower— Ike wanted his Army to be able to roll quickly from coast to coast—the Interstate Highway System is one of the great public work projects in American history, a tribute to faith in the power of government spending to achieve broad societal benefits. A half century later, more and more of the limited-access, multiple-lane highways being built to relieve the pressure of urban and suburban chokepoints are privately financed, a throwback to the for-profit turnpikes of Colonial times.

Washingtonians heading west out of the nation's capital to the horse farms of Middleburg and Upperville and to the exurbs beyond have three choices: the slow but direct U.S. 50; Interstate 66, almost certain to be a crawl at rush hour; and the "Greenway," a lightly traveled, privately owned and maintained, for-profit stretch of Virginia Route 267 that for a stiff fee allows customers to breeze the 14 miles between Dulles International Airport and Leesburg. The toll, which began at $1.75 when the Greenway opened in 1995, has been rising roughly every 18 months and is expected to hit $4.80, or roughly 34 cents a mile, by 2012. In Indiana, Governor Mitch Daniels, a former Eli Lilly & Company executive and George W. Bush's first budget director, led the charge to lease the state's only toll road to Australia's Macquarie Infrastructure Group and Cintra SA, which paid $3.85 billion in return for all toll and concession revenues for 75 years, an almost complete reversal of the spirit of the Interstate Highway System. As always, efficiencies and cost-benefits were cited to justify that transaction, as if there were no value in having the public retain responsibility for a public thoroughfare.

Of all the peacetime obligations of government at all levels, education is the most profound, the most pressing, and the one most enshrined in our history and national stories. The access to good schooling lies at the heart of the meritocracy—whether it's Abe Lincoln studying by candle-light in his Kentucky log cabin or Colin Powell rising up through the public schools of the Bronx and the City College of New York to become the first African American to serve as chairman of the Joint Chiefs of Staff and as Secretary of State. Yet today, when so many urban public schools are clearly in a state of collapse, when even a blind pig could see that city after city is basically warehousing its poorest and most vulnerable children to keep them off the streets from 8 to 3, when no one can deny that the gap in resources between mostly black inner-city public schools and mostly white suburban ones grows greater by the day, the little debate that is raised and the few solutions put forward are couched almost solely in economic terms. "Competition," we are told, will save the schools, whether in the form of charter schools, proprietary education corporations such as the Edison schools, or outright public grants and tax breaks to those parents who choose to educate their children in private or parochial schools.

I don't dispute that competition has its place—in schools, in roads, in hospitals, even in prisons. Complacent bureaucrats can always stand to be shocked into new thoughts and fresh action. But some things, by their very

importance, should be immune from purely economic
solutions. That is rarely how it is in these times. The public
sector gives, the private sector gets. Corporate America's
share of our national income booms—from 7 percent in
mid-2001 to 13 percent in 2006. Its share of our national
tax load dwindles. (In 1995, the ratio of withholding—or
payroll—taxes to corporate taxes was three to one; by 2002,
the ratio had widened to five to one.) And economic reasoning becomes the only reasoning allowed at the table.

Something changes when government ceases being the
service provider. The compact between citizen and state
erodes. A model based on mutual obligation—services from
the state in return for such citizen-services as participating
in the national defense through the military draft—yields to
a sales model. Everything has a price point.

The transition is rarely abrupt. It is more a whittling away.
The seemingly efficient customer-service modalities of the
private sector replace the sometimes maddeningly slow
ones of the public sector. True, everything might not be
entirely satisfactory. Complaining to a consumer-affairs 800-
number might be less immediately rewarding than writing a
letter to your congressman, but at least there is now a range
of possibilities in personnel and price not available in a
system of public delivery. In time, the patient, the student,
the driver, the ''client,'' the ''customer'' adjusts to a new,
cost-effective way of doing things. Life goes on, but there is a
loss. A sense of connection to our national institutions dims
until it finally begins to vanish altogether.

The reverse is equally true. Something fundamental also
changes when the people broadly writ cease to serve the
government and the national interest, when functions once
thought of as being fulfilled largely through civic duty
are instead turned into contractual relationships. That

change, too, is gradual—it's an erosion by inches, 1. or miles—but the effects are deeply felt.

Of all the undertakings of government, war-making is most solemn, and of all the challenges of the presidency leading the country into war and building the political consensus to sustain it through conflict should be the greatest. Lincoln is remembered today more for his stirring words than for the deftness of his political skills, but it was the combination of both that held the deeply divided North together during the four bloodiest years in our national history and preserved a Union that a lesser president might have seen dissolve.

More than three decades later, Admiral Dewey sailed into Manila Bay, commencing the United States' involvement as a global power and adding a further challenge to the president's war-making portfolio: persuading a fundamentally isolationist populace not just to risk the ultimate treasure of young Americans' lives but to do so on foreign shores. The 1915 sinking of the *Lusitania*, the "atrocities" in Belgium, and the decoding of the Zimmermann telegram were all part of the mystique by which Woodrow Wilson managed to lead a deeply hesitant nation into World War I. The Japanese attack on Pearl Harbor, Germany's declaration of war on the United States, and our own subsequent declarations of war on Japan and Germany rendered moot Franklin Roosevelt's deft maneuvering around the popular aversion to taking up arms again, for a cause thousands of miles removed across a seemingly unbreachable ocean. Korea—a "police action," not a war, since U.S. forces fought under the United Nations banner—and Vietnam raised similar issues, and required of the president similar leadership skills and sleights of hand. (As sneaky as it was, the Gulf of Tonkin resolution engineered by Lyndon Johnson was arguably no more fraudulent than invading Cuba to

"Remember the *Maine.*") Always through it all there was resistance, sometimes organized, sometimes anarchistic, to overcome—from the violent Civil War-era "draft riots" led by Irish immigrants in New York City to the violent campus upheavals of the Vietnam era that came to a head tragically at Kent State University on May 4, 1970.

Indeed, the essence of being an American citizen was the insistence on being personally involved when warfare was to be unleashed in our name, even if that meant being involved in the streets. Part of that was civic duty, but the exercise of civic duty on the eve of war was always colored by the reality that the military draft would draw combatants from broadly across society. If our forces were to be led in the field by a professional class of warriors trained mostly by the service academies, the trenches and the holds of the troop carriers banging ashore would be filled with citizen soldiers, men and now women who had laid down the pleasures and responsibilities of peacetime lives to defend us from peril.

No more. The all-volunteer army—which is to say, the paid contractual army—ended that connection. We still care when we hear or read about the new American dead and wounded in and around Baghdad. We grieve for their families and honor their sacrifice, but for most Americans—and particularly for the most influential—this newest war takes place largely on television. Relieved of the responsibility for fighting it, spared the necessity of sending our sons and daughters into combat to honor a civic duty, we are equally relieved of the responsibility of taking to the streets to protest a war launched with lies and mismanaged virtually from the moment American soldiers arrived in the Iraqi capital. Draft dodging at least compelled attention to what one was dodging. The absence of a draft plus the primacy of economics allows freshly minted MBAs to convince themselves they are serving their country by pulling down six-figure bonuses at Goldman Sachs just as surely as they would be by pulling guard duty in Fallujah. In his disingenuous simplicity, George W. Bush recently made explicit that we could not be involved in the Iraq War if we did not have a volunteer army. It is perhaps one of the most astute things he has ever said.

Hiring people to fight wars removes the discipline of requiring political credibility and building political support. War no longer needs be limited to cases in which the populace will affirmatively support the risk of what is precious to them. When the president talks today of sacrifice, he is referring to a financial deficit the importance of which is understood by nobody and risk of life by persons who have been paid for that eventuality or, to put it more honestly, have been advised that such may be part of the bargain by which they receive a college education.

Thus, Iraq becomes the epitome of the corporate state. Everything can be purchased; it is only a matter of amount and terms. Private contractors—the second largest army in Iraq—are not parties to the Geneva Convention. Any moral content to action is subsumed in the marketplace. Even war is simply a matter of finding the market price for persons willing to risk their lives. This not only removes an essential discipline on executive governmental power; it also undercuts the legitimacy of action by the United States.

When I reflect on how I would act if my three draft-age grandchildren were to be called to risk in Iraq, I am humiliated by the poverty of my involvement in the current crisis. The reality that we have created a system of financial inducement for individuals to fight our wars has diminished the quality of citizenship, maybe the most extreme example of the extent to which the language of economics has changed the country in which we live.

At bottom line, what an econocentric view of the world most breeds is arrogance. History, literature, philosophy, even law—they all beget gray areas and revel in fine distinctions. Economics, though, is quantifiable, or so it pretends. Instead of philosophers, it breeds winners and losers. The winners strut; the losers take the suckers' walk. Bullies rule the day. The oversized "Mission Accomplished" sign that greeted George W. Bush when he landed on the deck of the *USS Abraham Lincoln,* just months into a war that has now gone on longer than World War II, was the equivalent of one of Terrell Owens' NFL end-zone antics, only less funny. Sadly, the scene was typical of the times: The arrogance is everywhere.

Consider these by now infamous quotes from two of the leading business figures of the day:

> "You know what the difference is between the state of California and the *Titanic?* At least when the *Titanic* went down, the lights were on."
> —Enron CEO Jeffrey Skilling, in a Webcast on the manipulated electricity shortages in California.

> "What used to be conflict of interest is now a synergy."
> —Stock analyst Jack Grubman, dismissing the idea that he might be too close to companies he was recommending to investors.

One doesn't have to read between the lines to hear the contempt for the weak, the losers, anything that stands in the way of profit, anything that's not, in economic terms, sexy. In one sense, that's not surprising. Big money and big deals have always attracted hard chargers and braggarts, but this particular form of hypercharged braggadocio seems determined to level everything that stands in its way.

An example: Without public debate or explicit government action, the United States has emerged in very recent times as a country without a pension system. Among financial instruments, pensions—by which I refer to defined-benefit pensions that promise to pay retirees a set sum annually, generally calculated as a percentage of final year's pay—are about as unsexy as money gets. Risk is low; the goal line clear. Prudence is both advisable and legally required. Yet for well over a century, these boring defined-benefit pensions were part of the bedrock of the American economy. Large corporate employers considered themselves responsible for providing such real pensions. Congress, too, gave clear indication of its ongoing support for such a pension structure back in 1974 when it enacted ERISA (Employment Retirement Income Security Act) legislation and created the Pension Benefit Guarantee Corporation (PBGC) to protect workers from employers who failed in or intentionally abused their fiduciary responsibilities. In concert, PBGC, ERISA, and the long tradition of a lifetime relationship between employer and employee *appeared* to assure most retirees of income security over and beyond the minimal protection provided by Social Security. I wrote *appeared* in the preceding sentence because at current rates defined-benefit pension plans will be as extinct as the dodo within a generation.

What went wrong? Some companies such as LTV Steel, Bethlehem Steel, U.S. Airways, United Airlines, Polaroid, and Kemper Insurance either defaulted on their defined-benefit pension obligations or otherwise walked away from them, leaving the PBGC holding the bag. As of September 2005, these pension-debt transfers to the federal government had left PBGC nearly $23 billion in the hole with another $108 billion in probable claims waiting down the road—figures so ominous that until very recently Congress was unwilling even to talk about a solution, much less proceed toward one.

What had once been a solemn obligation became instead just another way to game the system. The airline companies would go to their employees and say, look, times are tough, we can't pay you any more money but we'll sweeten the pensions. Then the executives would extract all the remaining value from the companies for themselves and let the airlines go under, knowing that PBGC would have to pick up the obligation. During my time with ERISA, I effectively headed up the Pension Board. I saw this time and again, and could do nothing about it. The gamers held all the cards.

Far more frequently, the management of American corporations has simply ceased offering defined benefit plans, replacing them—if at all—with contributions to a defined contribution plan, which is simply a fancy name for a savings account. Notices of these switchovers inevitably praise the economic benefits. When IBM announced in 2006 that it was repudiating its remaining defined-benefit plans, a spokesperson estimated that the move would save the company as much as $3 billion through the next few years, while providing it with a more predictable cost structure.

Employees, too, are invariably assured they will be better off without Big Brother—or Big Blue—stuffing their piggy bank for them. Defined-benefit plans have pokey rates of return that leave employees at the mercy of inflation. Better that they should become their own financial planners, the masters of their own retirement fate. Not only do defined-contribution plans represent a continuing gift from management—typically something along the lines of matching 25 to 50 percent of employee contributions up to a maximum of 5 or 10 thousand dollars; they also allow, even compel employees to choose what instruments to invest in from among a smorgasbord of offerings, again typically within a single family of funds. In effect, they force market literacy on the working populace at the same time that they create a forced relationship between the employee and whoever is behind the family of funds available for investing. Congress has obliged this rush to defined-contribution plans by legislating its own buffet spread of tax-deferred savings and retirement accounts, from 401(k)s to Roth IRAs—an array that dovetails nicely with Corporate America's determination to rid itself of defined benefits.

On the surface, all this would seem to be both a great boon to the bottom line and an unalloyed triumph of economic entrepreneurialism. The former is certainly true. Corporations get to rid themselves of a burdensome ongoing obligation that they can then book as an instant profit, thus increasing earnings, market valuation, and—perhaps not coincidentally—the value of outstanding stock options.

For employees, though, things are not so simple. Leave aside the question of whether workers will save for their retirements on their own. The evidence—including a negative national savings rate for 2006—suggests otherwise, but that's not my point here. Ignore also, at least for the moment, the macroeffect of reducing the employee-employer relationship to short-term, wham-bam-thank-you-ma'am affairs, the paradigm that IBM and so many others have worked hard to create. My guess is that such a model is going to end up saddling the federal government with hundreds of billions of dollars in additional costs since failed investors have never been strong on retirement planning. But the issue goes beyond that as well.

The reality is that, no matter how generous the matching funds under defined-contribution plans, they transfer risk away from the corporation and onto employees. (Simultaneously, and providentially from government's point of view, risk is being transferred away from the battered PBGC, which doesn't concern itself with defined-contribution plans.) The further and more critical reality is that the greatest benefits of transitioning away from real pension programs accrue not to present and future retirees but to the financial-services industry, which helped plan and execute the transition in the first place. Instead of every worker becoming his own financial manager under this new dispensation, every worker *needs* a financial manager. That truly is the point.

Congress got into this act as far back as 1975 when, in amending the Securities Act, it declared fiduciary relationships a "commercial asset" and thus managed the difficult feat of monetizing trust and destroying it in any real sense at the same time. But in its own deeply deferential and well-lobbied way, Congress was only anticipating the spirit of the times, the rising pressure of financial conglomerates, and the overweening desire of service providers for more leeway to deal with themselves.

This effort reached its apogee three decades later, in August 2006, with the passage of the Pension Protection Act, yet another Orwellian name in a subset of legislation overwhelmed with them. For most of its 800 pages, the new law purports to be a rescue operation for the Pension Benefit Guarantee Corporation, but along the way it manages to further shred the already tattered understanding of a fiduciary relationship. Henceforth, transactions between service providers to a pension plan and the plan will be permitted so long as the service provider is not a fiduciary to the actual assets involved in the transaction and so long as the plan receives "adequate consideration" for the deal—that is, (the transaction must be priced at the same value available in a publicly traded market. For deals that aren't traded in a market, a fiduciary would make a good-faith judgment of the fairness of the transaction under rules the Department of Labor (DOL) is supposed to produce. If history is any guide, most transactions will be structured so as not to be congruent with markets; the DOL regulations will be long in preparation and ultimately will defer to the facts and circumstances of individual situations; and the service providers will exploit monopoly access to this gigantic assemblage of assets.

This was never the original intent of ERISA. Indeed, I remember so well the response of the late Senator Jacob Javits of New York, one of the fathers of the legislation, when he was asked at a 10th-anniversary symposium on ERISA whether he could support loosening the statutory prohibition against related-party transactions. Javits thought about the question over lunch, then came back with an unequivocal answer: "No" he said, "we must keep the prohibited-transaction provisions. We are dealing with a very great evil."

The most well-meaning of the architects of the evolving pension landscape dream of independent and expertly governed funds through which workers will secure their retirement savings and emerge as a new legitimate base for corporate power. That is the opposite of evil, but in the real world, poorly governed pension funds in the control of agents with their own agendas, inevitable conflicts of interest, and the ability to dominate law making and administration have no hope of providing the legitimacy that was the promise of the pension dream. The roughly $9 trillion in equities held by institutional funds—nearly two-thirds of total outstanding equities—makes them too large a beast by far for the financial-services industry to leave alone, and predictably they haven't.

What used to be a relatively simple business of providing goods and services to the pension marketplace now has morphed into a second and superior one—at least in terms of wealth creation—of providing financial services to the owners of the first. Consultants fall out of trees despite their high cost and doubtful contribution to the economic welfare of the enterprise because they provide pension-fund trustees with protection against the possibility of liability and any claims of negligence even as they disengage trustees from their fiduciary tasks. (I didn't do it; the consultant did.) Let in the front door, consultants double-deal by the back one, producing investment products that they sell to the funds they are supposed to be monitoring.

A 2002 audit of Hawaii's pension fund revealed that its consultant recommended 16 money managers over time and that 14 of them were paying the consultant for so-called marketing advice and other services. That is an extreme example but not a singular one. Pension consultants meanwhile migrate from offering advice to selling in-house funds in which they advise their clients to invest to going into the management business themselves, and as they do, the ethical lines further blur and disappear. Yet who can blame them? They are only following the money, and there is so much of it. At least one of these consulting companies was sold for in excess of $1 billion; the principal of another famously bought a rather expensive extraterrestrial flight.

The SEC was following the money with a more weathered eye back in 1958 when it unsuccessfully opposed allowing a funds-management company to issue public stock. Back then, if so rarely today, it could see the writing on the wall. Congress, for its part, was not only following the money but facilitating it when it approved Section 25 of the Securities Acts Amendment of 1975, and thus in effect overruled the legal opinion of Henry J. Friendly of the U.S. 2nd Circuit Court of Appeals, one of the finest judges of the twentieth century. Henceforward, with the willing help of Capitol Hill, an investment advisor could receive any and all profit on the transfer of its business without incurring liability to the company or its shareholders. And thus the modality of trust—an inveterate and unchanging code informing the management of property for others without the manager being allowed to make personal profit—was transformed into a commercial mode, a relationship entered into for profit.

No one involved in approving the legislation seems to have noticed (or if they noticed, bothered much to care) that when the manager is authorized to pursue personal profit, the owners' interest is no longer the sole object of management, as the old spirit of the law had it. Rather, owners are merely the incidental beneficiaries of the management's pursuit of enrichment, and what enrichment it is! Similar logic, in another age, might have landed its proponents in a madhouse.

Almost no one seems to have paused to consider either that by allowing market makers and market players to become one and same, companies like Goldman Sachs were basically handed the keys to the U.S. mint. No longer did they have to sit on the sidelines while the principals wheeled and dealed. Now they could wheel and deal themselves, but with a decided advantage since they, as market makers, were often privy to advance knowledge of the principals' intentions. In essence, cheating was legalized, and investment banking became the Cheaters Ball. (Former Goldman Sachs CEO John Whitehead, I should add, could see this coming and opposed his company's going public for all he was worth.)

The elimination of any compelling fiduciary considerations has launched vast financial energy, to be certain; but that energy most often expresses itself in the maximization of service charges levied against the various trust funds. Some charges are disclosed, many are not, although the mutual fund industry probably produces more numerical data, more comparative analysis, and more sheer paper than any other financial sector. The industry is fond of citing an expense ratio that it claims to be in an average range of 1 percent. But as Jack Bogle and others have shown convincingly, expense ratio data tends to conceal more than it reveals. For starters, expense ratios represent only about one-half of the true cost of owning mutual funds. Hidden portfolio transaction costs and sales loads likely double the typical cost of equity-fund ownership, raising it from 1.4 percent to as much as 3 percent of assets, according to Bogle's 2005 book, *The Battle for the Soul of Capitalism.* Bogle's conclusion: In 2004, investors paid costs estimated at $72 billion. What's more, from 1997 to 2002, the total revenue paid by investors to investment banking and brokerage firms exceeded $1 trillion, and payments to mutual funds exceeded $275 billion.

Is that opening up the financial markets to the wonders of unfettered capitalism? Or has it all been a setup for what amounts to old-fashioned legal theft? The answer is probably a good deal of both, but at least when the victorious Viking raiders plundered the treasuries of medieval France, they were forced to come through the front door.

Jack Bogle, in fact, is the perfect role model for how fund managers and funds should conduct themselves. For a quarter century, from 1974 when he founded the Vanguard Group until he relinquished his board membership in 1999, Bogle effectively allocated all his firm's profits to the benefit of Vanguard's shareholders, forgoing billions of dollars of personal wealth in pursuit of his deeply held convictions. Those principles were laid down another quarter century earlier, in 1949, his last year at Princeton, in what must be one of the most magisterial senior theses of all time:

- To place the interests of fund shareholders as the highest priority;
- To reduce management fees and sales charges;
- To make no claim to performance superiority over the stock market indexes;
- And to manage mutual funds, "in the most honest, efficient, and economical way possible."

As Bogle told a House subcommittee in April 2004: "These goals proved to be closely aligned, not only with what I regarded as the *spirit* of the Investment Company Act of 1940, but with its *letter:* to insure that mutual funds are 'organized, operated, and managed' in the interest of share-owners, rather than of managers and distributors." So successful has Bogle been that Vanguard is not only the world's lowest-cost provider of financial services but one of the world's two largest mutual-fund firms.

Later in his testimony, Bogle returned again to the 1940 Act, after noting that 36 of the 50 largest fund-management companies were owned by U.S. and foreign financial conglomerates, banks, brokerage firms, and insurance companies. "These businesses purchase fund companies in order to earn a return on *their* capital; yet the 1940 Act makes earning a return *on the fund share-holder's* capital the over-riding priority. This rarely acknowledged conflict of interest cries out for study." Indeed it does, along with so much else.

Wall Street's most highly developed skill, it is often said, is renaming old products so as to justify collecting new and higher fees. Certainly that's true of the so-called economic liberation of pension funds. By renaming and repositioning savings accounts, the financial-service sector has reaped huge rewards. It is true as well of hedge funds. Not one in ten thousand people really knows what a hedge fund does besides providing customers some sort of nuanced improvement on the old practice of risk taking in various investment decisions, but everyone can admire the fee structure: 2 percent, plus 20 percent of profit.

So it is also with private equity. The idea is an old one, tracing back at least to a widely circulated article by Michael Jensen that appeared in the September-October 1989 issue of the *Harvard Business Review*. Titled "The Eclipse of the Public Corporation," the article spelled out the efficiencies of having an incentivized management owning a substantial share of the upside risk and profit. Jensen's idea never really died out, but today it finds itself flush with cash (some $2 trillion in buying power), heady with big-name deals (Hertz, Duncan Brands, Universal Orlando, Equity Office Properties Trust, Domino's Pizza, Staples, J. Crew Group, Neiman Marcus, RJR Nabisco, and Toys "R" Us have all been taken private in recent years), and bathed in the sort of blue-chip respectability that only mighty success can bring. George H. W. Bush, former Secretary of State James Baker, and ex-British Prime Minister John Major are advisors to one of the most successful private-equity firms, the Washington-based Carlyle Group, while Massachusetts governor and Republican presidential candidate Mitt Romney is among the founders of another, Bain Capital. The profit allure of private equity has become so vast that it, not investment banking, is where the very smartest and most aggressive kids are flocking today. Unable to resist the smell of so much money, global giants such as Goldman Sachs are entering the game as well, even though they are in some cases placing themselves in direct competition with their own customers.

Stripped of high-sounding rhetoric, private-equity firms have the same broad goals as the corporate raiders and junk-bond kings of two decades ago: buy underperforming companies at bargain-basement prices, restructure management, spin off parts if applicable, and sell for a staggering profit. Michael Milken wanted no less, but unlike his modern counterparts, Milken had to operate mostly in the broad light of day. Taking companies private frees the new owners of most public disclosures, including their own drawdowns from the corporate till.

High-sounding rhetoric, though, never strays far from the private-equity movement. Henry Kravis, who has emerged as one of the premier financiers of the age and perhaps private-equity's foremost spokesperson, likes to talk about the fiduciary nature of privatized management.

"If you examine all the major corporate scandals of the last 25 years, none of them has occurred where a private equity firm was involved," Kravis told a New York audience. "Businesses have failed under our ownership and that happens. But to my knowledge there has been no systematic fraud or management abuse in our industry. Why? Because I believe that as general partners we are vigilant in our role as owners and we protect shareholder value. The private equity industry should be proud of this record."

Kravis goes so far as to raise the prospect of a dual equity market—one dominated by private equity, in which there is excellent governance and close attention to the fiduciary obligation of running the company for the benefit of the owners; and the other composed of the public market in which the interests of shareholders are subordinated not only to those of managers but also to the many conflicted service providers with access to the corporate cash flow.

Maybe that will happen although I have trouble seeing to whom private equity's wildly incentivized entrepreneur/ managers are going to sell their enhanced value holdings if the public-market sector is to be as degraded and riven as Kravis suggests. How are options to be priced in the shuttered world of private equity? How are bonuses to be calculated in the absence of a market price? If the dichotomy between the well-governed private market and the conflict-driven public markets persists, won't investors ultimately consider publicly available holdings junk stock?

Questions like that deserve to be chewed over. Indeed, they almost demand to be chewed over—the implications for corporate control and shareholder democracy are too great to ignore—but for the moment, here is just one final fact. Even with generous allotments from his board of directors, Roberto Goizueta of Coca-Cola needed an entire business lifetime to become the first billionaire employee in American history. (In fact, two Coca-Cola directors told me on separate occasions 10 years apart that the Board had *never* acted to approve Goizueta's compensation or retirement. This was pure self-pay.) Eddie Lampert, whose ESL Investments has amassed a fortune privatizing Kmart, Sears, and other failing retail giants, earned more than $1 billion in 2005 alone and James Simon earned $1.7 billion in 2006. That, I suspect, truly is the point of the whole exercise. It almost always is.

Chapter Eight

RETURN OF THE BLOB

There is a model readily available for encouraging good corporate governance—an investment management company that oversees a pension fund with more than $80 billion in assets, as well as other funds that choose to avail themselves of its services. This company employs some 40 people—a virtual army—with no other brief than to worry about the governance practices of the companies being considered for investment. Do the directors and principal executives of these corporations take the long view—on environmental issues, on matters of public health, in terms of the relationships they're building and the friends and enemies they are making? This sounds like do-goodism. To an extent, it is just that. But it's enlightened do-goodism. Today's power play on pollution, on global warming, on energy can be tomorrow's public relations and revenue disaster. What's more, this form of do-goodism pays a clear premium: The investment company in question has significantly outperformed the relevant indexes year after year.

Another gaping difference between this company and most others in the same business: Not only are its annual profits available as an offset for required payments to the pension scheme, but all increases in the value of the management company—in the event it would be put up for sale or even if its market value as a private company would be recognized by the actuaries—are assets of the pension and therefore further security for the beneficiaries.

This is a company that makes a bundle of money, a company whose returns are envied by the industry, and yet it is also a company with a demonstrable heart. It is a company with a practical social conscience that puts the wealth creation of its beneficiaries above the wealth creation of its own managers. Its name: Hermes Investment Management Company. Hermes, in turn, is owned by the British Telephone Pension System, which is overseen by trustees from both union and management ranks of the British Telephone Company. (When the company was privatized two decades ago, Hermes went private with it.)

What makes Hermes so special? Part of it certainly is the general culture of the country of origin. The English are as capable of venality and greed as any other people, but for the most part, it is simply not considered good form for a CEO to be ruthlessly, 24/7, hard-charging and trampling everything and everyone in the path of wealth creation. That's the Yanks, they're apt to say in the cushier clubs of London, and while they might admire the bank balance of a Lee Raymond or a Bob Nardelli, they are reluctant to openly imitate them.

British law, too, enshrines shareholder rights in a way that would be unthinkable in the United States. Under Great Britain's Companies Acts, the most recent being 2006, publicly held businesses incorporated there must convene an emergency general meeting when 10 percent of shareholders so request, and all directors are subject to summary removal at that time. Virtually every advanced country in the world has a similar statute—another way in which the United States stands sadly apart in corporate governance.

(In testimony before the House Committee on Finance on March 8, 2007, Business Roundtable President John

Castellani basically dismissed the U.K. system as entirely unsuited to the United States, citing the dominance of state law over federal law on this side of the Atlantic, the greater percentage of "independent" directors on U.S. boards, and NYSE requirements that listed companies "have a mechanism for shareholders to communicate with directors, which provides shareholders a means of sharing their views with respect to executive compensation." It's a wonder Castellani's nose didn't grow Pinocchio style as he testified.)

Mostly, though, what makes Hermes special is its long-time CEO, now retired, Alastair Ross Goobey. Lean, well-tailored, and a fine musician, Ross Goobey looks on paper to be a prototypical English public-school product, and indeed his resume drips with establishment credentials: Trinity College Cambridge, special advisor to Conservative chancellors Nigel Lawson and Norman Lamont, author, top-level investment professional. Yet at the core, Ross Goobey is a determined nonconformist. With the support of virtually no other institution in the City—as financial London is known—Ross Goobey managed to create a style of activism that is now universally copied and practiced.

Ross Goobey waged a single-handed campaign to change the standard provisions of executive employment agreements. Before his campaign, departing executives routinely enjoyed a three-year "rollover"— they walked out the door guaranteed another three years of their current salary. With patience and persistence, Ross Goobey changed that to one year, a backpedaling on compensation that would be unthinkable in the current climate in the United States.

As the chief executive officer of Hermes, Ross Goobey also has been hell-bent on improving the governance climate. Since large institutions such as his necessarily invest the preponderance of their assets in marketable securities, so he reasoned, the integrity of the securities market on a long-term basis is a critical issue. Ross Goobey therefore committed Hermes to hiring not only expert investment strategists but also business professionals capable of analyzing and understanding which companies could be improved through greater oversight by their owners. To pay for this additional and often untapped expertise, Ross Goobey went to other large institutions and said, "Invest in my fund, and it will make you money." They did; the fund performed as promised; and because returns have long been superior, fees and profit participation have made activism profitable for Hermes.

At the end of 2006, the London Business School, along with three colleagues, finished a detailed analysis of the Lens Focus Fund's first five years of operation. The conclusion: This openly activist fund that welcomes and responds to shareholder power outperformed the relevant FTSE Index by 5 percent.

All of this has earned Ross Goobey bragging rights not just as the creator of great wealth for his employer but as the founder of shareholder activism in the United Kingdom. Thus, it was both surprising and deeply ironic that, at the Fifth Annual Conference of his marquee fund, Ross Goobey should have found himself in a fiery shouting match with one of the stalwarts of American shareholder activism, William Lerach.

The issue at hand was the courts and corporate governance. In his speech to the conference, Lerach urged British institutions to use litigation as part of their investment policies. The courts, he insisted, were the most efficient route for forcing shareholder democracy on reluctant executives and boards. That was too much for Ross Goobey, who surprised just about all the 300 or so people present by leaping to his feet and letting loose on the guest speaker.

To an extent, Ross Goobey was only reflecting a general European disdain for American-style class-action suits, with their huge contingency fees for the winning lawyers. That disdain has turned to fear in recent years as aggrieved American shareholders have used the U.S. courts to move against overseas corporations. As I write, shareholder suits are pending in New York against Parmalat, the bankrupt Italian dairy giant, and in Alaska against BP over its nine-figure payout to departing CEO John Browne. (In the Parmalat case, Ross Goobey's reluctance to litigate was over-come when Hermes became the lead plaintiff, but Hermes could not bring itself to engage Lerach to act as counsel.) In 2005, Ahold, the Dutch retailer, agreed to pay $1.1 billion to settle yet another shareholder class-action suit. Increasingly, too, European legislatures are opening the way for similar court actions, but without punitive damages and with caps on attorney fees. Ironically, German lawmakers approved class-action legislation at the request of Deutsche Telekom, which was facing some 2,500 separate lawsuits by share-holders upset by its collapsed stock price.

Certainly, that was part of what got Ross Goobey going, but I suspect his sharp reaction was also personal. His professional life has been devoted in large part to showing that, at least in Europe, corporate governance can be improved by more subtle pressures than shareholder suits. To his mind, Lerach was advocating using an axe when a scalpel would do better. That was probably enough to set him off, but he wasn't alone in taking offense. Ross Goobey and Lerach's verbal warfare had seemingly reached its peak when Ralph Whitworth, perhaps the premier American activist investor and a San Diego neighbor of Lerach, jumped in on the Brit's side: Litigation is all about money for the lawyers, Whitworth told the crowd. It has lamentably little to do with recovering actual damages for shareholders.

The debate, which raged until the moderator decreed a recess, wasn't for the faint-hearted. Neither side was used to yielding its points or the floor. More than anything, though, this set-to between three men with so much in common and so much common ground between them—men who have shared many podiums and panels over the years—was a telling comment on the health of corporate governance in the United States and on the gap between the American model of shareholder power and global standards.

Bill Lerach didn't have to come to London to pick a fight. His penchant for seeking solutions in the courts has made him feared and loathed in corporate boardrooms all across the United States. Lerach rose to national prominence during a 20-year collaboration with attorney Mel Weiss. Starting in the 1980s, the two essentially created the industry of shareholder litigation. Between them, Lerach and Weiss have taken on Enron, Dynegy, Qwest, WorldCom, and AOL/Time Warner in high-profile suits, as well as Michael Milken and savings-and-loan scandal poster boy Charles Keating.

After dozens of courtroom successes, Lerach had an epiphany: Monetary penalties alone were never going to change America's existing corporate governance scheme or provide owners with an effective means of protecting themselves and their companies from abusive practices. Lerach thus began to structure his settlements so that companies not merely would pay off the various parties in the litigation—lawyers, shareholders, insurance companies—but would also be required to transform their governance systems. In the process, he has turned the U.S. courts into an honorable, sensible, and more effective recourse for American shareholders than federal legislation, SEC activity, New York Stock Exchange rules, or state law amendments. Among the reforms that have crept into corporate best practices through Lerach's imaginative litigation is direct nomination of directors by shareholders—a simple step that has proven to work to everyone's advantage.

Ralph Whitworth has been no slouch either. Trained as a lawyer like Lerach and equally loathed in CEO circles,

Whitworth can claim plenty of good-governance successes of his own, but he is cut from different cloth than Lerach, with a decidedly different lineage. A Westerner born and bred, Whitworth came of age under the tutelage of maybe the most legendary rogue investor of them all: T. Boone Pickens. A wildcatter in his early days, Pickens transformed the American oil business through his attempted takeovers of Gulf, Phillips, and Unocal. After these efforts landed him on the March 4, 1985, cover of *Time*—pictured as a cowboy gambler in a high-stakes game—Pickens picked up the shield of William Jennings Bryan and began a populist campaign for president by organizing the United Shareholders Association.

Throughout, Whitworth was Pickens's loyal and competent agent. Whether it was battling the SEC or protesting state legislation that kowtowed to corporate demands, the combination of Pickens's money, Whitworth's skills, and tens of thousands of United Shareholder members created the possibility of a genuine ownership society. Among Whitworth's victories was authoring a petition that, in 1992, resulted in a major overhaul of the SEC's shareholder communication and compensation-disclosure rules. He also won regulatory changes that freed dissident shareholders from having to put forth an entire slate if they wanted to challenge only one or two nominees to a board of directors. Both victories sound technical, but for owner-activists these were major leaps forward.

United Shareholders dissolved in 1994, but Whitworth didn't give up the fight. Two years later, in 1996, he launched Relational Investors with backing from the massive California Public Employees' Retirement System (CalPERS). In the years since, Relational Investors has used pressure on directors and concentration of resources—its $7 billion in assets are invested in only nine companies— to fix underperformers from Waste Management to Home

Depot and Mattel. When necessary, Whitworth has stepped in himself to take over a board chairmanship. Despite a general aversion to seeking relief from the courts, he also brought in the white-shoes law firm Sullivan and Cromwell to help him do battle with the directors and top management of Pennsylvania-based Sovereign Bank, a brush with respectability that has helped to bring legitimacy to the entire field of investor activism. Most important, Whitworth has shown that hands-on attention can pay big rewards. Over its first decade of operation, Relational Investors has averaged an annual return of about 25 percent.

The struggle for shareholder democracy can be a blood sport. The 1995 Shareholder Litigation Reform Act—yet another misleading name—tried to put Lerach out of business by significantly raising the level of specific information, and thus advance expenses, necessary to bring a lawsuit. In 2007, under pressure from federal prosecutors, Lerach pled guilty to obstruction of justice, a charge that said far more about the Bush administration's ties to corporate America that it did about Lerach's courtroom practices. As for Ralph Whitworth, he was once labeled a "socialist" by the CEO of General Mills, a man presumably with little training in history or economics.

Another of the lone warriors for good corporate governance, Eliot Spitzer, has equally earned the enmity of Big Business and its establishment hit men. During one round of intense negotiations, a Wall Street investment bank lawyer tried to scare Spitzer off with a warning worthy of a *Sopranos* episode: "Eliot," he reportedly said, "be careful; we have powerful friends." The veiled threat wasn't likely to have much effect on someone who had previously broken up the real-life Gambino crime family, but it does hint at the stakes everyone is playing for.

Spitzer occupies a different place in the pantheon of shareholder-democracy heroes. As varied as Lerach,

Whitworth, and Ross Goobey have been in their approaches, they all managed to do very well for themselves financially, while also doing great good for their investors and for the real owners of the corporations they went after. For Spitzer, the gains have been largely political. In November 2006, he rode his assault on the boardrooms of America's corporations into the New York State governor's mansion. Almost certainly, he harbors hopes beyond Albany, and if he can continue to generate a flood of favorable media attention by attacking the greed and cronyism to be found on Wall Street and across the corporate landscape, he might just get there.

Yet as powerfully as Spitzer's meteoric political rise speaks to the public's longing for someone willing to take on Big Business and its excesses, the fact that he managed to accomplish with a relatively small staff what huge agencies like the Securities and Exchange Commission (SEC) and the Department of Labor have been unwilling to confront, even in the face of statutory requirements, says even more about the state of corporate governance and about the challenges that lie ahead.

Elected New York's Attorney General in 1998, Spitzer made the most of two advantages his office offered: a broad investigative and prosecutorial mandate under New York's General Business Law and the fact that Wall Street is located in his territory. Just a few years after taking office and with a staff that included volunteers from local law schools, Spitzer used his powers to investigate a number of high-profile financial scandals. While similar inquiries by both the SEC and the Congress had failed to gain traction, Spitzer successfully sued some of the nation's and world's highest-profile investment banks for inflating stock prices and colluding with affiliated brokerage firms to give biased investment advice. As a result, in 2002, ten firms—including Deutsche Bank, Goldman Sachs, and Salomon Smith

Barney—paid $1.4 billion in compensation and fines. Additionally, new rules and enforcement bodies were created to govern stock analysts and to insulate brokerage firms from investment bank pressure.

A year later, Spitzer zeroed in on mutual fund brokers who were giving select clients special trading privileges, including "late trading," in which investors could file trades at the previous day's price after the markets closed; and "market timing," which allowed these same privileged investors to buy and sell shares more frequently than allowed under the fund's rules. In effect, these practices allowed a small group of investors to profit at the expense of other shareholders in the fund. Through a number of prosecutions, Spitzer both forced reforms and secured more than $1 billion in fines and remuneration for investors. In all, he was able to ratchet down management fees within the mutual-fund industry by as much as 6 percent, still enough to yield obscene profits but at least less obscene than they otherwise would have been.

All this has brought inevitable comparisons with another New York governor and antibusiness crusader who later became president, Teddy Roosevelt. Spitzer doesn't run from the analogy. "Is there anyone today who doesn't accept what Roosevelt did?" Spitzer asked an audience of financial analysts back in 2003, in a 45-minute address that also included criticisms of the SEC, Wall Street, New York Stock Exchange Chairman Dick Grasso, the Bush administration, and the idea that corporate America was even capable of self-regulation. ("An abject failure," Spitzer called the self-regulation movement, in large part because so many proponents of the free-market system don't live "up to their own principles.")

Certainly, there are echoes of Teddy Roosevelt in that, but the point to be made here is that Spitzer or any other modern-day crusader shouldn't have to channel the TR of yore. Roosevelt operated in a world without the SEC, which didn't come into existence until the Great Depression; essentially without a Department of Labor, which was born in 1903 as the Department of Commerce and Labor and didn't gain separate status until a decade later; and without all the other regulatory instruments available today. Give Eliot Spitzer all credit for fighting the good fight, but he wouldn't have to work so hard if the regulatory structure hadn't failed so miserably.

I recall meeting with the voluble Harvey Pitt, back when he was still chairman of the SEC, and complaining in jest about the vast significance the commission had placed on a new requirement contained in the Sarbanes-Oxley legislation that requires CEOs and chief financial officers to personally certify their companies' financial statements.

"Harvey," I told him, "as a director of public companies, I have been certifying financial statements for the last 20 years. What's the big deal?"

His reply was quite serious. "Bob, this time we really mean it."

But they don't. The 70-year-old federal scheme for protection of investors remains a structure in shambles. Blessed through the years by the service of many dedicated professionals, the SEC has become an advertisement for the mandatory sunset of government agencies. In fairness, the elements of the SEC's failure are inevitable in any system that has corporations as participants. Business interests are today extremely effective at lobbying both the president—the SEC's boss—and Congress, which controls its budget. This pincer movement has compromised even the best of those picked to lead the SEC. Arthur Levitt, a profoundly principled man who served as chairman from 1993 to 2001, has described the agony of being pressured in connection with the Commission's review of accounting for stock options. And Levitt is hardly alone. The constant threat of withholding appropriations whenever the Business Round-table can round up a minimum of congressmen to rattle their swords cripples morale and creates a culture inimical to effective prosecution. Even when the SEC does dare to buck business interests as in the 2007 case of *Charter Communication vs. Motorola and Scientific American,* it is likely to find itself opposed in the Supreme Court by its own masters, in this case via an amicus brief filed by the U.S. Solicitor General.

As bad as the SEC's record has been, it is a shining star compared with that of the Department of Labor (DOL) whose regulative approach could be out of a Joseph Heller book: There is no problem; there is no reason to find out if there are problems; even if there were a problem, DOL doesn't have legal authority to deal with it; even if Congress provides the authority, DOL should not investigate; in addition, DOL has already looked into this problem.

A review by the General Accountability Office analyzed DOL's enforcement of voting rights of the estimated 100 million people with interests in employee benefit plans. The conclusion: DOL trailed all other enforcement agencies and even found excuses for not taking action. For evidence, look no further than the blatantly illegal collusion between Hewlett-Packard and Deutsche Asset Management described in Chapter 2. The SEC has at least completed an enforcement action in the case, but not DOL, which should be the lead agency in the matter. More than seven years after the fact, Labor continues to sit on its hands.

An April 1986 Senate report on DOL's enforcement of the Employee Retirement Income Security Act told the same sad story of incompetence. The report was the work of the Subcommittee on Oversight of Government Management of the Senate's Committee on Governmental Affairs, chaired by Maine's Bill Cohen, one of the few members of Congress then willing to take on the intellectual rigors of securities law and the hostility of established business interests. Among the conclusions: "Despite the millions of workers and retirees dependent on ERISA-covered pensions . . . the Department of Labor's implementation of the law has been characterized by grossly inadequate resources, longstanding deficiencies, frequently changing and inconsistent leadership, and shifting enforcement strategies." As part of ERISA's frequently changing leadership and as one of those who testified before the subcommittee, I saw all that close up and in living color.

So it goes. No wonder conflicts of interest mutate so easily into "synergies." Save for people like Ross Goobey, Bill Lerach, Ralph Whitworth, and Eliot Spitzer, so little stands in the way of Big Business writing the rules, poisoning the political and regulatory process, and—once everyone on the other side is sick, dead, or just plain exhausted—grabbing the whole pie.

Because they are not much good at hitting moving targets, lawyers, economists, and legislators tend to regard the corporation as a static enterprise to which fixed rules apply. Judges persist in basing their opinions about corporate functioning on historical conceptions or more recent theories such as the "nexus of contracts" or "natural entity" even though doing so dangerously ignores the present reality of this modern creature of business.

The nexus of contracts theory, for instance, focuses on the agreement between the two parties involved in incorporation: (1) the directors and officers, and (2) the shareholder/owners. As theory, that might be fine, but in practice this view of corporate existence fails utterly to take into account the situation of those not party to the contracts—"externalized" people who likewise have slim chances of reimbursement if they are affected by "externalized" events such as massive pollution.

Additionally, the "nexus of contracts" approach holds that the various laws regarding incorporation provide only an approximate framework of the bargain between the two parties. This thinking develops the vocabulary of "principal and agent" in describing the relationship of directors to the owners of corporations. Again, in theory that might be all well and good. In the real world, though, the common law of agency requires that there be explicit agreement between principal and agent as to the scope of responsibility in the relationship.

What's more, in the real world, the theoretical connection between owners and agents that "nexus of contracts" proponents point to as lending legitimacy to corporations barely exists at all. In the United States, shareholders do not nominate directors. Uniquely in the world, they have virtually no power to replace them, nor can they instruct them how to run the business. While many states may appear to guarantee these basic rights of ownership, the ability to exercise them is often subject to a convoluted series of parentheses. In Delaware (Section 141(k)), state law provides that shareholders may remove directors but then immediately limits the scope of this provision by denying shareholders the authority to call a special meeting unless the charter expressly permits it. Nor can shareholders in most recent times organize a sale to more satisfactory owners against the will of the incumbents. Far from being the guarantee of ownership rights, proxy contests for the most part make a hash of them.

The "natural-entities" theory is more high-minded nonsense. The idea that corporations should be afforded the legal status of flesh-and-blood human beings would have struck the Founding Fathers as sheer lunacy, but a series of

Supreme Court decisions has so expanded the concept that corporations now find themselves armed with the right to participate in the electoral process by contributing whatever money they see fit to influence public opinion and, through public opinion, the voting. Not surprisingly, Big Business has used these rights and its almost limitless collective resources to entrench and protect itself by routinely applying political pressure on those lawmakers who define the scope of corporate activity as well as the work of executive agencies in administering those laws.

Simultaneously, the traditional legal limitations on CEO power have evaporated. This is not coincidental: Creating the modern personhood of corporations only legitimates the idea that control and management can be separated from ownership. This assumption has also spread to the exercise of power by the directors and officers. Corporations today effectively make their own rules and funnel national resources in increasing volume for their own ends—a process quite accurately described as "corporate welfare"—with almost no regard for the outside consequences of their actions. This is a new form of energy in American life: a legally constituted structure of vast reach and scope that is accountable only to those who manage it.

To recapitulate, today's model of the large publicly held American corporation comprises five key elements:

1. The board of directors and chief executive officer are a self-perpetuating class removed from ownership monitoring or control.
2. The CEO dominates the selection process for new directors and for his own successor. The CEO can use corporate funds (and the potential of the corporation as a future client) for legal, accounting, political, and public-relations purposes if there are any challenges to his authority.

3. The corporate hierarchy, most notably the Business Roundtable, has become virtually interchangeable with the highest levels of electoral and appointive government office.

4. The corporation, through the CEO, has the constitutionally protected right to participate in electoral processes—whether elections or referenda—with virtually no restraint on the money employed; and the corporation has only the most limited need of the marketplace to raise capital.

5. Most large corporations generate more than enough cash for their needs; many have been buying back stock for years. Compensation plans are written to be enriching irrespective of stock price levels. There is, therefore, little marketplace discipline over corporate performance.

Such a powerful energy, so carefully designed to be self-perpetuating and so resistant to the normal restraints of a democratic society, should scare us all. The modern corporation's tremendous dynamism runs circles around our traditional language and legal categories as well as the current enforcement mechanisms that are based on these traditions.

The image that keeps coming back to me is one of those B-grade horror movies of the 1950s, a grainy, black-and-white, made-on-the-cheap double-feature filler with a title something like *The Blob That Ate the World.* Traditional weapons—tanks, armies, even atomic bombs—can't stop it. In the end, the job of saving the human species comes down to a few haggard scientists working feverishly in an underground lab to find a point of vulnerability as the Blob inches ever nearer. And then, just at the last moment, with the ooze pressing at the door, one of the scientists has a revelation: "We've been looking at this thing through the wrong lens. We've been assuming it's human, assuming that it's like us, and looking for its weak points that way. But it's not us. It's ooze. It's the Blob. We have to find some other way to think about it, to talk about it!" With that, suddenly, the solution is at hand. The Blob makes horrible shrieks. It groans, it thrashes mightily, but in short order it disappears, the sun comes out, our hero scientists emerge from their bunker lab to find humanity miraculously restored, and the credits begin to roll.

That is what I think is going to happen with this modern corporate monster we have allowed to grow among us. It won't be quick. The credits aren't going to be filling the screen anytime soon. But as with the fictional Blob, we will come to realize that natural entity— personhood—is the wrong metaphor for understanding the corporation. Corporations aren't that, and they aren't Frankenstein-like creations either, or unstoppable, profit-seeking missiles operating under the stealth of human guise.

Corporations are better described as "complex adaptive systems," designed to change in response to signals and to adapt to the environment in which they are placed. The trouble is that the only signals the modern corporation receives are slash-and-burn economic ones—an information flow that drowns out legitimacy and fiduciary considerations even as it encourages modern corporations to seek power externally while centralizing their own power base. By correcting the signal flow, we can restore the potential that has always been innate within modern capitalism and its chief agent, the large publicly held corporation: the capacity to create wealth for both owners and society in general.

The Statement of Principles on Institution Shareholder Responsibilities recently developed by the 10-year-old International Corporate Governance Network is one such attempt to correct the signal flow by expanding the understanding of the rights and responsibilities of true economic stewardship. (The statement can be found in the Appendix at the end of this book.) I could cite dozens of more examples. The woods are full of them.

Ross Goobey and Hermes have been beating at the same door. Through his insistence on good governance and responsiveness to shareholder concerns—and, critically, through superior returns on investment—Ross Goobey is steadily altering the environment in which Big Business functions. Corporations want to live; they'll adapt accordingly. In their own way, with blunter tools, Bill Lerach, Ralph Whitworth, and Eliot Spitzer have been doing the same thing—forcing directors and chief executives to listen to a broader array of voices, if only to protect their pocketbooks and stay out of jail. What the four men have in common is simple. Unlike the bureaucrats of the Labor Department and the SEC, they have skin in the game. Ross Goobey, Lerach, and Whitworth have all developed business plans based on the assumption that accountability generates real value. Unlike even the heads of the SEC and other regulatory bodies, Spitzer not only had direct personal authority to commit while he was New York's attorney general; he also had the voters' mandate behind him—and has an even greater mandate behind him now that he is governor, and a greater incentive if he aspires to still higher office. These things matter. CEOs have no trouble committing to the preservation of the corporate status quo. Those streets are lined with gold. Advocates for shareholder democracy and for good corporate governance need to match the short-term greed of the executive suite with some good old-fashioned enlightened greed of their own. That's what gets the beast's attention. That is language the corpocracy can understand.

As recently as a decade ago, doing battle against the entrenched power of corporations was a lonely business.

That is no longer the case. The excesses of Big Business, the overwhelming hubris of CEOs, their open disdain for any sort of accommodation with shareholder-owners, the unwillingness of some of the largest companies to even recognize the fractured externalities outside their corporate doors—all these factors have forced attention precisely where the Business Roundtable and its allies would least like us to look. As that attention turns into action, it sends a different set of signals to the complex adaptive creature called "the corporation," and slowly—so slowly it's hard to see it except in time-stop photography—the beast has begun to turn.

Chapter Nine

THE GREAT AND THE GOOD

How do we keep the corporate beast turning toward daylight? I'm convinced that the large institutional funds need to lead the way. They have the clout to make themselves heard in a world that respects nothing so much as raw power. The pension funds especially have an obligation to take the long view in their investment strategies. For them, *sustainable* wealth creation is the issue. In Ross Goobey and his Hermes group, other large institutional investors also have a ready example of how integrating management goals and owner goals can lead to rewards well in excess of the general market.

The Norwegian Government Pension Fund has many of the characteristics of the twenty-first century's ideal shareholder. It is large, its capital is dedicated "forever," the political traditions of the country are disciplined, and it is expertly managed. Created to preserve for future Norwegians equivalent value to that of the crude oil now being extracted from the North Sea—and formerly known as the Petroleum Fund—the fund is looked on as a pool of permanent capital, part of the country's patrimony, a resource to be husbanded.

To that end, trustees have decided that investment of what is now in excess of $250 billion can be best achieved in a diversified portfolio of equity securities of publicly traded companies—but not just any securities. An independent ethics council, originally imposed on the fund by the Norwegian government, has banned, among other companies, makers of land mines, cluster bombs, and any sort of nuclear weaponry.

As a result, the fund had to divest itself of at least 17 holdings, including Lockheed Martin, General Dynamics, and Britain's BAE Systems. According to Knut Kjaer, the extraordinarily skilled and literate executive director of the fund, the blacklist hasn't gone unnoticed. Kjaer told the *Guardian* that a number of foreign ambassadors had approached him on behalf of corporations either wanting to get off the list or avoid getting on it.

The ethics guidelines cover traditional corporate governance as well. The fund is required to "actively exercise its ownership rights." In 2005, that meant voting on more than 20,000 resolutions put forward by the 3,200 odd stocks the fund was invested in. Most were run-of-the-mill calls—approval of auditors, reelection of directors—but some were not. Kjaer has taken a particular interest in exorbitant compensation schemes.

"In principle, we like linking performance and pay," he said in the same *Guardian* interview, "but you will find us voting against the sort of deals where you see companies giving huge bonuses on historical performance. It must be real, linked to future performance, and over a reasonable time horizon." He also has opposed "any kind of poison pill" that seeks to prevent shareholder-initiated takeovers and acquisitions. Individual shareholders can rant and rave all they want about such matters and still be met with blind stares and deaf ears, but when the second-largest fund in the world—after only the Japan's Pension Fund Association—speaks, even corporate crowned heads must at least nod in its direction.

The Norwegian Fund operates within a unique structure. The *Storting*, as the Norwegian parliament is known, is the ultimate source of responsibility and authority. With the Ministry of Finance, the Storting decides the basic questions of what categories of assets to invest in and what percentage of the total portfolio each should comprise. But these bureaucratic layers don't impede results. The fund has produced excess returns of about 0.5 percent over the benchmark indices. What's more, the fund is almost universally admired. When the New Zealand Green Party recently lashed out against the managers of that nation's Super Fund for investing in weapons manufacturers and abusive employers, it used the ethical standards of the Norwegian Fund as its own bright line for responsible management.

The Norwegian Fund hasn't abandoned the language of economics. It is not a social justice fund dressed up as something else. Rather, the Fund and its managers have expanded economics to include issues long considered noneconomic in the boardrooms and executives suites of nearly all the biggest U.S. companies. That is a powerful step forward. The simple reality, though, is that while the Norwegian Fund and other overseas-based investment entities can point the way toward meaningful change in corporate governance practices, they can't compel it.

The United States is both the seedbed and the seat of the imperial corporation. It is where corporate hubris was born and bred, where it is most nurtured and sustained, and where the fight must ultimately be waged if it is going to be won. That means the best-managed and wealthiest institutional funds in the United States—outfits such as the Bill and Melinda Gates Foundation and Harvard University's endowment fund, with billions and billions of dollars at their disposal—bear the ultimate responsibility for taking the lead. They have the economic and political leverage; they already occupy the high ground of public respect. Their track records alone compel attention, in the only language Big Business really understands: Harvard's endowment has returned roughly 20 percent annually since 1990. Given that the endowment now totals roughly $30 billion, that's a new fortune being thrown off annually.

If being dropped by the Norwegian Fund can embarrass an arms manufacturer like Lockheed Martin and drive other investors away, imagine the shock waves that might pass through a boardroom or an executive suite if a company were blacklisted for bad governance practices by the endowment for the nation's leading university or by a fund that bears the name of one of the world's richest and best-known men. And imagine the effect if the Gates Foundation or the Harvard endowment, or better still both in tandem, openly denounced the pay packages granted to Bob Nardelli, John Snow, or Henry McKinnell—this is a list that truly can go on and on.

Irrational and excessive compensation practices are not going to be materially changed by disclosure or independent compensation committee members. Consultants are going to continue being hired at exorbitant expense, and they are going to continue to deftly select "peer companies" so as to assure the highest pay possible for their clients and for themselves. Like it or not, that's the way of the vast bulk of the corporate world. Indeed, the reason I have been rejected for service on so many such committees is likely that I have been regarded as *too* independent. Compensation reform will occur only if the largest institutional shareholders—and it would take only a few—demand a fresh look at the whole system.

Think, too, how other institutional investors would coalesce around such actions, and how invigorated the shareholder activism movement generally would find itself. *Lancet*, the British medical journal, was absolutely right when it editorialized on the subject in early 2007: "While it is naïve to assume that the action of a single investor, even one as large as the Gates Foundation, can effect substantial change, the actions of many investors—be they individuals, pension funds or large foundations—can do a great deal to improve the practices and policies of companies.''

No one, I think, can contest the impact such a stand would have. The effect would be more than riveting. It would be defining. What's missing is the will: The good must become the great, and that has yet to happen. Why? Why is it that in a world of blatant corporate excesses, an era of obscene CEO payouts, intelligent people with a proven penchant for astute analysis and a clear mandate to benefit the public, won't step up to the plate? Odd as it might seem, I think part of the answer can be found in an old gag:

> Two economists are walking down the street when one spots what looks like a $100 bill lying on the ground. As he stoops to pick it up, the other economist says, "Don't be ridiculous! If that really were a $100 bill, someone else would have picked it up."

The joke is stale, but the point remains. In the world that economists posit—the one they dress up with endless statistics—the most rational course of action has already been taken, whether it's grabbing money off the ground or, in the case of large institutional investors, pressuring Big Business to mend its high-hat ways. Hence, the hundred-dollar bill isn't real because it hasn't already been snatched up. Hence, too, the fact that Harvard, the Gates Foundation, and other U.S. megainstitutional investors have yet to exert serious pressure on corporations to address their governance failures proves either (a) that the failures don't exist or (b) that it is not in the investors' best interests to do so.

The owners and managers of these vast funds tend to couch such reasoning in more exalted terms. Harvard has perfected what could be called the "ivory silo" model for investing: In order to focus on education and, equally, to avoid offending any of the university's many vocal and often very well-heeled constituencies, the university endowment tiptoes around responsible engagement with portfolio companies.

In a series of open letters published between 1979 and 1987, then-university President Derek Bok spoke of the many pressures to employ Harvard's endowment on behalf of the leading issues of the day—ending apartheid in South Africa, improving race relations in the United States, supporting free speech, and others—and laid down the position that the endowment has basically followed ever since. The roots of that position can be found in Bok's 1979 treatise, *Reflections on the Ethical Responsibilities of the University to Society*:

> As I have already observed, society respects the autonomy of academic institutions because it assumes that they will devote themselves to the academic tasks that they were established to pursue . . . This does not mean that the universities should refrain from trying to influence the outside world. It does mean they should exert an influence by fostering the reasoned expression of ideas and argument put forward by their individual members *and not by taking institutional steps to inflict sanctions on others.* Universities that violate this social compact do so at their peril. They cannot expect to remain free from interference if they insist on using their economic leverage in an effort to impose their own standards on the behavior of other organizations. [Emphasis added.]

Basically, that boils down to the joke previously cited: If it were rational to use stock divesture to improve society,

Harvard would have already done it. Like Harvard—from which he dropped out after two years to write language for a computer-in-a-kit known as the MITS Altair 8800—Bill Gates and his wife, Melinda, simply want to be left to the business of giving away their money, without worrying about governance practices of the companies that keep refilling their pot of gold. Gates Foundation CEO Patty Stonesifer caught that spirit in her January 14, 2007, letter to the editor of the *Los Angeles Times,* responding to an article critical of the foundation's shareholder passivity: "While shareholder activism has worthwhile goals, we believe a much more direct way to help people is by making grants and working with other donors to improve health, reduce poverty, and strengthen education."

The ground doesn't get any higher than that. Who doesn't want to concentrate on doing well, especially when forcing corporations to do good is so entangling? To an extent, it's unfair to even raise these issues where Harvard and the Gates Foundation are concerned. They are demonstrable forces for betterment in the world today. As the old saying goes, you can't blame Columbus because he wasn't Magellan. That said, though, even the Gates fortune is not inexhaustible. Without replenishment—that is, without a robust return on its investments—the fund will find its philanthropic work compromised, perhaps even its obligations unmet. As with Harvard's governors, so with the Gates: They depend for their good works on markets performing to their maximum potential. That cannot and will not happen without empowered shareholders nourishing corporations and, if necessary, forcing ethical leadership on them.

The record is by now clear and the evidence overwhelming: Left to their own devices, without effective regulation, with no moral checks and balances other than cosmetic self-imposed ones, *and* without institutional pressure to reform, most corporations—and the largest among them—will loot their own resources to enrich the very few at their helm, ignore such externalities as pollution and global warming that are virtually certain to circle back to bite them from behind, and thus deplete shareholder value and in time drag the market as a whole down with them.

What I'm advocating is something different from Socially Responsible Investing, all in capitals. SRI is a noble cause and a welcome recognition of the responsibilities of corporate ownership. For the conscience stricken—and there is much to be stricken about these days—SRI mutual funds can offer the comfort of knowing that your 401(k) is not helping to hold up the stock price of a bad corporate actor. The SRI spirit can be found in the Norwegian Fund's blacklist, the flap over the New Zealand Super Fund, and elsewhere. But for all its virtues, SRI is hemmed in by limitations.

For starters, it is not, nor can it be, a substitute for lawmaking. Even the most well-intentioned, most elaborately researched conclusions of the best people—be they corporate executives, university professors, or philosophers—cannot achieve the importance or rise to the legitimacy of many people acting through democratically elected governments to effect change.

There is also the question of how effective an SRI focus actually is. Nelson Mandela certainly applauded those funds that refused to invest in companies doing business in South Africa during the dark days of apartheid, but the Nobel Peace Laureate equally applauded those companies that continued operations in South Africa in an effort to improve racial working conditions there. Indeed, the greatest difference between those who rushed to divest themselves of South Africa-related holdings and those who held on to them seems to be that the former suffered huge losses that their owners ultimately had to bear. Roland Machold, formerly the much respected investment manager for the New Jersey pension funds and later New Jersey treasurer, estimated his funds' losses at half a billion dollars.

For me, though, the largest problem with SRI is its passivity. Socially Responsible Investing is an act of omission, rather than one of commission—a refusal to engage, rather than an effort to change corporate culture from inside. As always, it's almost impossible to know the consequences of a road not taken, but when it comes to attacking egregious management and slipshod or worse governance practices, the consequences of the taken road are there for all to see.

Look at Enron and the United Kingdom's Marconi, where the noninvolvement of shareholder-owners allowed top executives to run rampant and ended up costing investors almost everything. Compare that, then, with how Warren Buffett seized direct personal control of Salomon Brothers at a time when the venerable investment house was being widely characterized as criminal, successfully negotiated Salomon's continued parole with the government, cleaned out the muck inside with the equivalent of a corporate backhoe, and ultimately realized substantial profits for all shareholders, himself included. Ralph Whitworth of Relational Investors did the same thing with Waste Management. In the face of stiff internal resistance, Whitworth engineered himself into the chairmanship of a company that was itself virtual waste, directed its recovery from massive accounting frauds, and reaped the rewards both for himself and for WM's continuing shareholders.

Although Whitworth and Buffett are both indisputable geniuses—Buffett has truly earned the sobriquet "Oracle of Omaha"—investor activism of the sort I'm advocating isn't about finding the "genius" solution to an ill-run enterprise. It is far more about preventing egregious mismanagement from destroying ownership value. You can't do that from the sidelines. That's a game you have to play to win.

We could probably more easily count the number of angels on the head of a pin than determine all the permutations and combinations of self-interest when that term is applied to something like the Gates Foundation or Harvard's endowment. Who exactly is entitled to the fruit of Harvard's endowment? It is not the donors of the property, for they are not investors in the corporate sense. Their gifts come, or should come, without strings. Yet the donors should also have some say in directing the yield of their gifts. Should it go to today's students? Today's faculty? The students or faculty of tomorrow? How about the Gates? Is their self-interest today- or tomorrow-directed? How much should they be committing now to curing devastating diseases in the most forlorn parts of the world if that means fewer resources to fight the same battle in the future when improved technology and medicines might be available?

As murky as all this terrain gets, the one element of self-interest that all parties can agree on is the need for a healthy equity culture—what Gus Levy of Goldman Sachs so brilliantly described back in the 1960s as "long-term greed." Such greed is not accomplished merely by paying excessive deference to Wall Street and the financial sector when the markets are on the upswing, any more than good personal health is accomplished by praising your doctor when you're not sick. Rather, a healthy equity culture depends on encouraging the conditions that nourish long-term growth.

Thanks to the United States's historically healthy equity culture, the real annual rate of return on corporate ownership has been approximately 6 percent over the past century. In comparison, bonds returned about 2 percent after inflation. Over just 25 years, the impact of this difference on a compounded basis is dramatic: An initial investment of $1 million put into equities will be worth $4.3 million, whereas bonds will return just $1.6 million. This same difference, multiplied by tens of thousands, can clearly shape whether a society is rich or poor. A healthy equity culture doesn't just create billionaires, although it certainly does that. It doesn't just swell endowments and foundation coffers and allow their managers to plan for a rosy future, even though it does that, too. A healthy equity culture promotes a wealthier overall society.

How do you create and sustain such a culture? Among many factors, equity markets need a fully articulated legal system that respects private property—precisely the factors that the economist Hernando DeSoto points to as lacking in the Third World's informal economies. Though the United States is recognized as having a relatively effective private-property system, this ownership is a two-way street, and nowhere more so than with the ownership of corporations. A fully realized equity culture depends on active share-holders. If owners decline to exercise their prerogatives, those rights will atrophy until eventually the shareholders find themselves as legally disempowered as Sao Paolo squatters. This is particularly true for massive, respected institutions. Shareholder capitalism in the United States today has been trivialized because the most learned institutional investors—the universities and the foundations—have conspicuously declined to be associated with the effort.

Equity culture is also promoted by a mindset that accepts risk and failure as positive factors. The United States, more so than Europe, has provided a system for "bold experiments," some of which will inevitably fail. Harvard, Bill Gates, and many others have all grown rich beyond measure by successfully playing the "risk" side of that equation. The enormous pool of money that their foundations and endowments collectively represent—the majority of equity in the

United States and the world—provide the bulk of the capital to continue the "bold experiments" that will, in turn, enrich those who fund them.

But all this is dependent on trust that capital markets will play fair; that information will not be withheld from investors; that CEOs won't raid the corporate treasury; that directors will exercise their fiduciary responsibilities; that regulators will not be in the pocket of the supposedly regulated. Let that climate of trust break down as it is in danger of doing today, and markets will not attach attractive values to listed companies, equities will back down toward or below the historic returns of the bond market, and the culture that has sustained a century of unmatched growth will come tumbling in on itself.

That is Argument One for institutional investors of the magnitude and scope of Harvard and the Gates Foundation getting involved in corporate governance: If they don't, they will ultimately pay the price, along with all the rest of us. Argument Two is simpler: Who else is going to do it?

The rush of new shareholders to the equities market over the past century has massively diluted ownership. Exxon-Mobil has, as I write, 5.73 billion shares outstanding; thus someone who held, say, a million shares—worth somewhere in the range of $75 million—would still have an ownership stake in the company of .017 percent, so fractional as to be barely noticeable. Even huge funds like that operated by Norway typically own no more than 0.5 percent of a company's total value. This atomization of ownership has been further attenuated as stock certificates have become registered in the names of nominees to facilitate transfer to custodians for security. On top of that, most corporations have made any substantive input from shareholders a long and expensive process.

All this is exactly as predicted by the late Abram Chayes, the corporation law professor at Harvard Law School who introduced me to the subject a half century ago. In his introduction to *Corporations* by the great scholar on the subject, John P. Davis, Chayes wrote, "Ownership fragmented into shares was ownership diluted. It no longer corresponded to effective control over company operations. Shares became investments, claims on earnings, themselves the object of ownership and of ready purchase and sale. They signified less and less a traditional owner's relation to productive assets. Business decisions gravitated to small boards of directors, the members of which no longer held office by virtue of major investments in the company, and which were under no significant outside control or supervision."

Adolph Berle and Gardiner Means were just as prescient 70 years ago in *The Modern Corporation and Private Property* when they advised: "We may grant the controlling group free rein, with the corresponding danger of a corporate oligarchy coupled with the probability of an era of corporate plundering." That, in essence, is where we are today: under the thumb of a corporate oligarchy, bent on plundering and unchecked by any effective ownership.

The question is: Who is going to do anything about it? Not regulators. They've proven their reluctance. Not Congress so long as the "personhood" of corporations allows them to distort the political process with their contributions. Not the executive branch so long as campaigning is massively expensive and CEOs and their allies are massively generous to candidates on all sides, just in case. (The prospect of an Eliot Spitzer presidency is, admittedly, tempting to contemplate in this regard.) Not the atomized individual owners except in the rare cases when a corporate activist with the resources of a Carl Icahn can force change or when a family trust such as the Los Angeles-based Chandlers can pull resources to shake an underperforming media giant like the Tribune Company by the teeth.

The only other group even empowered to change the corporate culture from within, directors, have repeatedly shown their reluctance to substantially question management. As former Fed Chairman Alan Greenspan pointed out, "Few directors in modern times have seen their interests as separate from those of the CEO, who effectively appointed them and, presumably, could remove them from future slates of directors submitted to shareholders." So much for the almost theological respect being paid to the concept of independent directors by places like the New York Stock Exchange. Directors of nearly all major U.S. corporations are self-perpetuating and thus cannot be held in any meaningful sense to be independent of the organizations on whose boards they serve. To paraphrase Abraham Lincoln, you can tell people that dogs have five legs, and perhaps even convince them it's true, but that doesn't change the fact that the animal has got only four.

At this point, alas, Greenspan throws up his hands and leaves corporations to the not-so-tender mercies of their CEOs in a spirit of *faute de joueurs*—win by forfeit. After all, to return to the $100 bill joke, if shareholders were a viable base for governance, they already would have chosen to exercise their rights. That's a questionable enough premise in its own right, but it also ignores laws that prohibit institutional owners from simply shrugging off their fiduciary responsibilities. Existing federal statutes respecting pensions (Employee Retirement Income Security Act of 1974), mutual funds (Investment Company Act of 1940), and banks all make it clear that it is contrary to both law and tradition for a fiduciary to be free unilaterally *not* to protect the value of trust property. In fact, employee benefit plan trustees are obligated to involve themselves in the affairs of portfolio companies to the extent that this involvement is necessary to preserve value.

The fact that such laws have been laxly enforced doesn't negate their underlying intent or the moral as well as legal imperative for large institutional investors to pay attention to them. Which brings us to the third argument why such investors need to involve themselves: No one has a greater obligation.

"There is no such thing as an innocent shareholder . . . ," the late Supreme Court Justice Louis D. Brandeis once said. "The person who has a chance of profit by going into an enterprise . . . should [not] have the chance of gain without any responsibility." To me, those words have greater meaning now than they did even in 1911, when Brandeis first spoke them in testimony before the Senate Banking Committee.

History will look back on the 1990s and early 2000s as a time when the principal officers of public American corporations transferred from shareholders to themselves approximately $1 trillion—or 10 percent of the market value of public exchanges. This must be the largest peacetime movement of wealth ever recorded, and it was accomplished through stealth that amounted to theft and in a spirit of regulatory permissiveness that certainly rises near to the level of criminal neglect. That is the hard and shameful reality of our times: We saw it coming, watched it happen, booked our profits, and did nothing about it until far too late. If we fail to learn the lesson from that, we'll only double our shame.

All of recorded history teaches us that vital societies are characterized by the informed and energetic participation of the members. The democratic myth depends on legitimatization through the consent of the polity. Corporations are simpler than nation states: Specific rules define the responsibilities of participants one to the other. Owners are assigned the position of ultimate recipient of corporate wealth after all contractual claims have been settled. Thus, owners have the incentive to assure that adequate property will exist to compensate their investment and risk taking. Of the millions of shareholders in a large corporation, however, only a few are well positioned to provide this sort of equity-increasing leadership, and so it falls to those few to rectify the current abuses of the imperial corporation and, in so doing, to assure that a healthy equity culture prevails.

Harvard—to focus in on the huge institutional investor I know best and have been trying to have this dialogue with for decades—is the very substantial owner of the publicly traded stocks of large businesses. Its president and fellows created the first and arguably most enduringly successful special-purpose investment vehicle, Harvard Management Company, to maximize the long-term value of its assets. Harvard Management is a fully competitive entrant in the field of money management and pays world-class wages to its professional employees. Through its Management Company, Harvard has become an owner of a vast span of enterprises whose collective functioning affects life on earth in profound ways. What then is the extent of Harvard's responsibility as owner? What is she doing now? Does she ensure optimum value? What should she do in the future? Instead of merely leading the field in extracting value from the market, should the fees already paid to Harvard Management Company be used to support a staff of specialists focusing on corporate governance and other activist ownership techniques that both protect and increase the fund's equity?

These are not theoretical questions for Harvard. Corporations and other institutions do not function in a discrete manner. Their interrelationship with society cannot be neatly defined by boundaries, either theoretical or practical. Harvard has developed a very worldly competency to increase the asset value of its investments. Can one seriously object to her taking worldly responsibility for some of the consequences of these same investments?

Institutions cannot simply define problems as being external to their mission and thus dismiss them. If they don't accept responsibility for what, after all, makes them rich—if they don't realize that long-term greed depends on nurturing the equity culture, not ignoring it—the university, its endowment, and its managers invite a chaos where the most difficult problems will be ignored by those best qualified to help and left to fester in the certainty that they will become toxic. Harvard, the Gates Foundation, and their kith and kin must face reality. Our great institutions don't exist in a tower, ivy-covered or digital. They live in the real world, where businesses have a costly impact and where the exercise of oversight duties is not just an option but a compelling necessity. If the best and brightest won't take a stand, who will? And if they don't take a stand, do they even deserve to be called that?

Ownership of tangible property is for the most part clearly understood. Right and responsibility for use are in balance: When the horse dies, you have to get rid of it. When ownership is dematerialized into shares of stock—or in more recent times, computer blips indicating shareholding—the concept of responsibility becomes elusive. Responsibility becomes even more elusive when it entails risk and expense that might not be directly compensated for by increased value. Multiply that, in turn, by the massive implications of having ownership of institutions whose success depends on taking risks held by institutions whose very nature requires minimization of risk, and it's easy to imagine conflicts of interest of debilitating proportions. The fact that there has been no enforcement of breach of fiduciary obligations either by the executive or judicial branches of government muddies the waters even more. The trend of some prominent judges toward the law and economics policy of efficient compliance favored by Douglas Ginsburg and others poses the question of whether the courts even intend to require compliance with existing trust law.

For all these reasons and more, former Stanford Law School Dean Bayliss Manning once conjured up a model of a new corporation without owners, reserving to some vaguely designated arbitration process the circumstances in which management's conflict of interest with the corporation's vestigial owners needed adjudication.

Economists, less prone to flights of fancy, have long insisted that the possibility of hostile takeover—acquisition of a controlling block of the outstanding equity stock—is the necessary discipline to assure that management power is exercised in the interest of owners and of society. The hard reality, though, is that hostile takeovers do exist and their ameliorating effect has been, at best, minimal. Corporate governance is a mess. The money grab is well advanced. The question isn't whether the current morass is self-corrective or whether fairy-tale ownerless ownership can work. The question, to put it in the idiom of large company shareholdings, is whether society can tolerate trust ownership without requiring that the inveterate fiduciary responsibilities be enforced. I hope that, by now, you can anticipate my answer.

There can be no genuine accommodation of corporate power and the public good in a free society until a language of accountability is developed that comprehensively, fairly, and effectively allocates costs and rewards. Laws must be based on information that is as full and accurate as possible. The books can't be cooked. Oversight has to be open and free. In a horse race, the owners' associations can't agree about much, but they can agree about inspections to be sure that the horses aren't doped. It would be not only sad but needlessly damaging to democratic society if the great and the good of the world's institutions could not do as much for the corporations in which they invest.

That is the crossroads we have reached. Harvard, the Gates Foundations, and all the others can choose to exercise their ownership obligations, or they can conclude that no action is a preferable course, a collective failure that would imperil the greatest wealth producer in history: the business corporation. They have the choice of imposing the language of accountability on the grazing land where they have grown so wonderfully fat—the common pasture of publicly traded stocks and the corporations that stand behind them. Or they can continue to exploit this common pasture without feeling any correlative obligation to contribute to its upkeep and sustainability, a choice that would in the last analysis be self-destructive.

Harvard, the Gates Foundation, and the others can choose to recognize the unmistakable reality of fiduciary relationships as practiced by the modern corpocracy: that these relationships largely don't exist in any meaningful fashion; that the flesh-and-blood status of corporations allows them to run roughshod over regulators and legislators; that in virtually all the financial conglomerate institutions that hold the preponderance of fiduciary authority today, the putative fiduciary has more valuable relationships with the company whose security it holds than with the beneficiary of the trust it is legally obligated to protect. Or they have the choice of continuing to ignore this as well, in which event the ultimate losers will be the small investors who will be left with crumbs after all the value has been stripped away through fees, bonuses, pay, stock options, and the other ingenious tools by which the rich of America get richer and richer.

There is a final choice as well. These great institutions of good, these protectors of intellectual integrity and ameliorators of human distress, can practice through their

investment policies the same sense of enlightened leadership they bring to their other spheres of influence, or they
can continue to turn a blind eye to the rot at the core of
what supports them. The great Jewish philosopher Maimo-
nides said it best nearly a millennium ago: "If not you, who?
If not now, when?"

Chapter Ten

STILL, I DARE TO DREAM

We live in the Age of the Imperial Corporation, maybe the only clear winner of the Cold War. Politically, the United States has had trouble adjusting to its role as the sole superpower. Across the Pacific, China begins to nip at our heels. Nearer to home, the European Union and its member nations grow reluctant to join American-led crusades. But capitalism suffers no apparent limitations. It is triumphant in the world today as is its prophet, the global corporation, and its religion, the language of economics with its apparent precision and impartiality. The accumulation of wealth has been agreed on as the principal objective of society. The corporate form of organization has been accepted as the most efficient means to achieve that objective. The role of Big Business in formulating public policy goes all but unquestioned. Power has been concentrated in corporations and, within them, with the Chief Executive Officer as almost never before. But note the "almost" in the previous sentence. We have, after all, been here previously.

Historians tell us that the human story tends to move in waves. A Great Awakening comes and goes and comes again and again with a metronomic regularity that you can almost use to set your watch. The same is true of markets, whether they are in tulip bulbs, New World real estate, or stocks. Irrational exuberance builds, prices climb to dizzying heights, and finally when the last sucker has been found, the bubble breaks to the general misery of all around, and soon—once the lessons have been forgotten, and that takes a surprisingly short time—the process starts all over again. Greed, it turns out, is like a supervirus. It might go dormant, it might mutate into another form, but it never dies out entirely.

The late historian and Kennedy confidant Arthur M. Schlesinger Jr. detected in American history a cyclical pattern of 30 years more or less between peaks of selflessness and peaks of selfishness—between asking what you can do for your country and demanding the country give it all to you. That being the case and assuming the present time has established a new standard in selfishness, maybe the best course of action is just to wait things out. What is 30 years in the long sweep of time? A blink.

Others, including *Fortune* senior editor Geoffrey Colvin, seem to think the shift away from selfishness is already under way. Look at new laws restricting the tax deductibility of CEO pay or at freshly coined SEC regulations requiring mutual funds to disclose how they vote the shares they own or at the variety of ways in which boards are now being infused with directors not wholly in the pocket of the chief executive. Why get in the way of the ship when it is turning in any event, and the tide is running in your favor?

My problem with such thinking is twofold. First, the vaunted reforms of recent times are either at the margins or, in the case of the push for independent directors, mostly hokum—cosmetic touches that fail to address the huge deficiencies in the underlying culture. Second, and more important, we can't afford to wait three decades for this current epoch of greed to self-correct, or two decades, or even one.

The generally robust market of the past several years has masked the deep erosion of trust that underlies all trading. Everyone wants to be in equities when the Dow Jones Industrial Average (DJIA) is stampeding above the 13,000 and even 14,000 mark, but bull markets turn around—they're cyclical also—and this time when the bears come out to play, there is going to be no avoiding the rust-ridden infrastructure the markets are built on. Investors will remember Enron and WorldCom, of course, but they also will recall Bob Nardelli's nine-figure payout; the deeply cynical full-page ads that Exxon has begun running, touting the company's heartfelt commitment to the environment; the fact that the Treasury secretary's job is all but a divine right of ex-Goldman Sachs CEOs; the outrageous money grab by the New York Stock Exchange's (NYSE's) own CEO, made the worse by the fact that Dick Grasso seemed to see nothing wrong with it; and the fact that through scandal after scandal and outrage after outrage, the regulators empowered by law to handle such matters for the most part sat idly by or actively subverted the existing statutes to serve Big Business's bidding.

When that happens, quite frankly, the bottom begins to fall out on the whole mess. One financial commentator, Steve Pearlstein of the *Washington Post*, saw just that happening in the 3.3 percent plunge in the Dow Jones Industrial Average of February 27, 2007. In a column the following day, Pearlstein noted that the DJIA nosedive coincided with word from Robert Steele, the Undersecretary of the Treasury for Domestic Finance, that the Bush administration still believes the best solution to market abuses is not improved government regulation but greater self-regulation, a utopian view belied by all the examples just cited.

As Pearlstein wrote, "This is precisely when markets need good regulators, and good regulations, to make these financial intermediaries behave in the 'rational' way that the Bush administration says they are supposed to. To leave it to 'voluntary' codes of conduct and 'market discipline' is both naïve and dangerous."

Maybe Steele's comments weren't a precipitating event to the plunge. Maybe it really was the skittishness of the Chinese financial markets that set off this American shock wave. Whatever the cause, the bottom line is that without trust, investors flee from the stock markets, capital becomes ever more dear to raise, expansion stops, growth reverses itself, and slowly—or maybe not so slowly—these great engines of wealth creation that we know as publicly traded corporations grind to a halt.

The market is already sending plenty of other clear signals that such a time is nearly upon us. More and more sophisticated investors such as the endowments of Yale and Harvard are opting not to invest in traditional securities listed on the public exchanges. A decade's experience has shown them that better returns at comparable risk can be achieved in other markets such as hedge funds and, particularly, private equity. Why? Why should it be worth the vast expense to take a publicly traded company private? Because as Henry Kravis has pointed out, that way the new owners can reform governance. They can toss the bums out if need be; they can rein in outlandish pay schemes and force the CFO to play fair with the books. In short, they can restore trust to the operation, and restoring trust pays big dividends.

The Corporate Library (TCL), an advisory firm based in Portland, Maine, has developed a technology to evaluate firms in terms of the quality of their governance. Unlike traditional rating agencies, TCL focuses on what managements do: Is the compensation system based on value conferred to owners? Are acquisitions and earned surplus deployed profitably? Is the accounting system aggressively inclined to maximize current earnings? By TCL standards, gaps as large as 5 percent can be attributed to governance differentials, more than enough to attract the smart money and reward it for its efforts.

The question, then, is how to accomplish the same end for companies that remain publicly traded. Not every company is going to be taken private; this is a trend that will turn, too. Nor should all corporations go that route. Private corporations retain their personhood. They get to corrupt the political process as surely as public ones if they so choose, but with less transparency in their operations. What's more, the rewards of their success flow to far fewer people. None of that is necessarily good for any of us.

Beyond that, as a practical matter, there always will be need for a public market. Even if a market is only the best of bad alternatives, it's necessary for setting value. Without a public market, mutual funds would have no reliable way to price their holdings. The large public pension funds aren't going to allow a public market to disappear either; if nothing else, politics won't permit the funds to abandon it. Too much rides on its existence. Corporations that issue shares to the general populace aren't going away. They just need to be governed better so that their owners, too, can reap the 5 percent bump that comes with better practices. How do we get there?

One way is by having business leaders who actually lead. There is no absence of would-be philosopher kings among the current crop of most-photographed CEOs, and no wont of journals and newspaper line inches devoted to their latest pronouncements, but there are too few examples like Frank Blake, who on taking over as CEO of Home Depot reversed the compensation package of his predecessor and conditioned his own ultimate compensation to depend 90 percent on creating value for shareholders. And there are far too few CEOs like Jeff Immelt of GE who actually do have something to say almost worthy of philosopher-king status.

In an interview with the *Financial Times (FT)*, Immelt not only came out against multiyear contracts for CEOs and for banning compensation consultants—two leading causes of excessive payouts—he also argued that, to motivate staff and avoid excesses, CEOs' pay should be kept within a small multiple of the pay of their 25 most senior managers. "The key relationship is the one between the CEO and the top 25 managers in the company because that is the key team," Immelt told *FT*. "Should the CEO make five times, three times or twice what this group make? That is debatable, but 20 times is lunacy."

Even more amazing given his title, Immelt seems to practice what he preaches. For 2005, he received a relatively paltry $3.2 million in salary and no cash bonus, well within the 2 to 3 times range compared with his senior team. Hold those figures up to the $198 million former Business Roundtable head Henry McKinnell received from Pfizer in 2006, after being dismissed from the CEO post because shareholders lost 40 percent of value on his watch. That truly is lunacy.

Satisfactory involvement by shareholders would readily exist if top management wanted to encourage it. Indeed, all the problems of governance (independence of directors, transparency of compensation, accountability for external liabilities) could easily be solved by CEOs who desire such a solution. Since that is not the case—since the Immelts are rare, the McKinnells are plentiful, and self-enrichment is the barely concealed principal objective of almost all top management—nonbusiness leaders in and out of government need to get involved. Of those, too, there is a serious shortfall.

A century ago, when business titans like John D. Rockefeller, Andrew Carnegie, and Cornelius Vanderbilt bestrode the nation like giants and J. P. Morgan served in effect as the nation's central banker, a countervailing force rose up composed of, among others, dedicated journalists like Ida Tarbell, Lincoln Steffens, and Upton Sinclair and supported by presidents Teddy Roosevelt and, later, Woodrow Wilson. (It was Roosevelt who gave the journalists their nickname, "muckrakers," from a character in Bunyan's *Pilgrim's Progress.*) Thirty years ago, when Big Business was again ascendant and reckless, Ralph Nader struck back against its abuses with two books, *Unsafe at Any Speed* and *Taming the Giant Corporation*, and with a series of inspired legal actions as well as his Public Interest Research Groups. Today's resurgent imperialists have almost no known enemies of great stature other than Nader, still going strong in his mid-70s; Eliot Spitzer; and the often lonely shareholder activists cited in Chapter 8. Spitzer, alas, cannot be cloned. That leaves regulators unwilling to regulate, congressmen whose silence has been bought and paid for, and presidents and presidential candidates loath to get on the wrong side of their biggest campaign donors.

The extent to which competing voices have been shut out of the American political dialogue—which in business matters is much closer to a political monologue—can be read in the sad story of the Commission on Presidential Debates. Created ostensibly to assure that the American people would have the opportunity to judge candidates for the nation's highest office in the crucible of public exchange, CPD is today largely financed by corporations and essentially owned by lobbyists. Contributions are tax deductible and donations can be kept private. Not surprisingly given such support, CPD has evolved from its lofty original goals into the chief protector of the two-party system and the main barrier to the introduction of any ideas into public discourse that stray too far from the accepted catechism.

In 1996, when CPD barred Ross Perot from that year's presidential debates, the *New York Times* editorialized that the commission had proved itself "to be a tool of the two dominant parties rather than guardian of the public interest. This commission has no legal standing to monopolize debates, and it is time for some fair-minded group to get into the business of sponsoring these important events." Undaunted and undeterred, the commission four years later barred Ralph Nader from participation although Nader was on the ballot in all 50 states and had been proclaiming an aggressive agenda of public reform over almost half a century. This is not democracy. Democracy is about debate; it's about the open flow of ideas. It's about *clogging* the brain waves with possibilities. This is democracy's evil twin: corpocracy straight and simple—government of, by, and for the corporations; not of, by, and for the *demos*, the people.

How we got here is no secret. This is a wide highway, easy to follow in retrospect. The broad entry of everyday Americans into the stock market in the decades after World War II atomized ownership of corporations just as they were maturing into the greatest wealth-making machines the world has ever seen. That vested enormous power in top management, specifically in CEOs. Through the Business Roundtable—and with the favorable legal climate that Lewis Powell helped to foster on the Supreme Court—CEOs increasingly focused their clout on the political process. Simultaneously, the triumph of modern economics and its cult of the quantifiable served to pare all public policy decisions down to a raw test of numbers. Cost efficiency, in turn, allowed government at all levels to abandon historic responsibilities and, as that happened, the citizenry gradually but surely abandoned the state. Into that vacuum, then, rushed the very interests that had done so much to create it until today even the political process is largely in the control of corporate masters who fund campaigns, back "debates," and stymie in every way conceivable their own regulation. Out-of-control CEO compensation is the symptom, the smoking gun, but corpocracy and the discontinuity it has created with our political traditions is the real disease, the ultimate reality.

This, in truth, is the perfect storm that Justice Byron White foresaw so clearly in his dissent in the Supreme Court's 1978 decision in the *Bellotti* case, granting corporations "personhood" to participate fully in the political process. His dissent, White wrote, was based on the simple and fundamental premise of "preventing institutions which have been permitted to amass wealth as a result of special advantages extended by the State for certain economic purposes from using that wealth to acquire an unfair advantage in the political process. . . . *The State need not permit its own creation to consume it.*" Again, the emphasis is mine, but Justice White clearly meant it to be his, too. Frankenstein, the Blob, out-of-control viruses—when it comes to describing the corpocracy, the metaphorical range is shockingly slim.

Still, I dare to dream. I have a recurring fantasy of a president in the not-distant future who sees this deep erosion of trust in corporations, stock markets, and the nation's financial life generally for the clear and present danger that it is; a president who understands the need to recreate the balance of accountability both within these vast wealth-generating entities and between corporations and the American polity; a president with the political and personal courage not just to talk about the threat but to act on it.

In my fantasy, this president convenes a meeting in the Roosevelt Room of the White House with the Secretary of Labor, the Attorney General, and the chairpersons of the Securities and Exchange Commission and the Federal Reserve System for the announced purpose of discussing the role of the corporation in the nation's affairs. The Roosevelt Room is not particularly large, but there's plenty of room in it for my dream dialogue. The president begins:

The voters are entitled to feel that they have "one government," which means that we will administer consistent policies and that they can rely on our constancy in the future. I have invited each of you as essential administrators of policies relating to shareholders of American companies. You all know that about half of all Americans are beneficial majority owners of virtually all of our publicly traded companies. Their rights are set forth in existing federal statutes. Each of you—Madame Secretary with respect to ERISA, Mr. Chairman with respect to mutual funds and the Investment Company Act of 1940, Mr. Chairman with respect to certain bank trusts—is responsible for administering trusts exclusively for the benefit of plan participants.

In recent years, there have been massive conflicts of interest. "Fiduciaries" acting pursuant to statutes for which you are responsible have flagrantly violated their trust status. Know that from this day forth, it will be the policy of this government that the obligation of fiduciaries under ERISA and the Investment Company Act of 1940 is to perform as owner of the portfolio companies in which they own shares—"exclusively for the benefit of plan participants." I have asked the Attorney General to attend this meeting so as to make clear that the full law enforcement power of this government will be deployed so as to ensure full and prompt compliance with these laws.

My dream, it turns out, is a miniseries because after this meeting, the president repairs to the Oval Office for a second get-together. This time, only two attendees are present. The president addresses them both:

Mr. Secretary of Defense and Mme. Administrator of the General Services Administration, the United

States government is a substantial customer, and it used to be said that "the customer is always right." Well, this administration intends to restore that ancient chestnut to its traditional importance. The whole procurement process is replete with concern over corporate conduct—from safety to antidiscrimination in employment to environmental concerns and on and on. You are both well familiar with that territory. However, there has been no focused attention on the potential impact of DoD and GSA as the world's largest customers on the totality of corporate governance. That is about to change.

We all acknowledge that the government has a wasteful, confusing, and expensive regulatory approach to contracting. The evidence towers over us. What better way to improve this process than by substituting good corporate governance procedures for existing controls? They are, after all, a form of accountability that is natural to corporate structure and energies, and not a set of rules invented and superimposed by government. So incentivized, the audit committees of the boards and shareholders could do some of the heavy lifting now being performed by federal investigators. They could help create the right corporate motivation, see to it that the right resources are allocated, and look for the right scalps if a company has to pay fines or is debarred.

"That," he concludes, turning to other business on his desk, "will be all."

Is what I fantasize utterly off the wall? Two meetings, no new laws—can things really be changed this easily? The answer happens to be yes. The framework is in place. The laws exist. Regulations abound. One president determined to right such primal wrongs can make a world of difference. Nor can it be considered executive branch meddling or destructive federal intrusion for government to set about undoing a situation that it created by determining that a majority of stock ownership would be held in trust form.

Look at the marketplace for the votes of American publicly owned companies. Institutions vote perhaps two-thirds of the total. Many of the so-called individual votes have traditionally been held in the nominee name of the appropriate broker to facilitate transfers, and these shares have as a custom been overwhelmingly voted for management, yet another massive impediment to governance reform. (After a flip-flop, the New York Stock Exchange appears to be ready to change the practice of permitting brokers virtually unlimited license in voting these shares, a procedural change that could have significant substantive consequences.) Large institutions, for their part, have freely indulged in stock lending among themselves to help secure desired outcomes in proxy fights, a practice that calls to mind a proposal by the imaginative money manager Dean LeBaron during the takeover wars of the 1980s that a formal market be created for the purchase and sale of votes. LeBaron was only semiserious—the direct purchasing of votes is plainly illegal—but it's easy to see why there remains massive confusion about who exactly is doing the voting and under what pressures and toward what ends. If these were political votes, government would tear the whole system down and start over again. The least it could do with these corporate votes that are vital to enforcing good governance practices is to assure that the playing field approaches level.

The fault, dear Brutus, as Shakespeare knew, is not in our stars, but in ourselves. What is required is political leadership at the highest level to compel accountability from business and to ensure that long-term ownership of enterprise is empowered. And that, of course, is what has been most sorely lacking, with rare and precious exceptions.

In addition to lone heroes riding to the rescue, we also need a legal structure that more accurately reflects the reality of corporate functioning in the United States—a structure that contains corporate hubris without strangling its remarkable talent for wealth creation. It is well to remember that the First Amendment to the U.S. Constitution was not meant to protect the Church from government intrusion, but rather to protect the government in its temporal responsibilities from the intrusions of the dominant institution of the day, the Church. We need similar protection today from the dominant institution of our own time, the corporation. Otherwise, it rules us as surely as the Puritans ruled Plymouth Bay Colony or the Crown once ruled England, not the other way around.

Failing new constitutional language—admittedly, a stretch given time constraints and the admirably complicated process for amending that great document—we need to somehow reverse the Supreme Court's incredible devolution from *Santa Clara County v. Southern Pacific Railroad* (in 1886) to *First National Bank of Boston v. Bellotti* almost a century later, a tortured path that took us from a lobbyist's notes on an opinion to Justice Powell's promulgation of a corporate constitutional right of speech. If there is a corporate right of speech, how about other creatures of government—does the Town of Cape Elizabeth, Maine, Sanitation Department have a right of free speech? Can the employees organize, advertise, and promote policies contrary to their elected supervisors? Do they have federal constitutional protection for this, notwithstanding any state law provisions about the limits of conduct of state officials?

This is legal reasoning so inane that it defies being satirized, yet serious questions that go to the nature of the American Experiment lie just on the other side. Can our democratic system even survive as long as corporations retain the constitutionally assured position of participants in the polity?

"Other than by redefining democracy, I do not see how it is possible to reconcile democracy with the practice of conferring on institutions the rights and powers of real persons," Charles E. Lindbloom writes in his 2001 study *The Market System*. "The rationale for democracy is rights and powers for living, hurting, and aspiring persons whose assigned rights and powers give them protection as well as opportunities to pursue their aspirations. It would make no sense, on democratic grounds, to assign such right to fire hydrants or computers."

Although the *Bellotti* opinion appears on its face sufficiently absurd as to suggest that reversal is just a matter of time—and even though its pernicious effect can be seen daily in the coercive corporate lobbying that neuters whole areas of public concern, from excessive fuel consumption to pollution, global warming, and well beyond—the juridical persistence of this doctrine suggests that patience will be unavailing. Perhaps, though, the court can be edged along. A state legislature, for example, can make a finding that corporate participation in election and referendum campaigns has created a risk of subverting free expression of the citizens' will. To that end, the following bill was filed in December 2006 for consideration by the Maine legislature in its 2007/2008 session:

LD 1507—An Act to Clarify the Role of Maine Corporations with Respect to Public Political Activities

BE IT ENACTED by the People of the State of Maine as follows:

Section 1. 13-C MRSA Section 302, first paragraph, as enacted by PL, 2001, c. 640, Pt. A, Section 2 and affected by Pt. B, Section 7, is amended to read:

Unless its articles of incorporation provide otherwise, a corporation has perpetual duration and succession in its corporate name and has the same powers as an individual to do all things necessary or convenient to carry out its business and affairs; except that a corporation may not take part in political debate or campaigns or support political parties or candidates except as specifically authorized by law, or participate in a public initiative or referendum on any matter that does not materially affect the property, business, or assets of the corporation.

SUMMARY This bill will clarify Maine corporation law to make it clear that corporate entities organized under that law are not entitled to exercise the political rights of natural persons or citizens. It is prompted by the U.S. Supreme Court decision in *First National Bank of Boston v. Bellotti*, 435 U.S. 765 (1978). That decision suggested that corporations, to the extent they are legal "persons," might enjoy certain political rights such as the right to participate in a public referendum on an issue not directly affecting the corporation's business. This bill makes it clear that while corporations may in the conduct of their business activities exercise powers similar to those exercised by natural persons, they do not thereby obtain the political rights of natural persons or citizens, such as voting, supporting candidates, or participating in referenda on issues not directly affecting their business activities.

Another piece of fantasy? Perhaps, but even such a modest step as this proposed bill could bring before the U.S. Supreme Court the possibility of overturning the illegitimate authority of corporate power that has been so destructively sustained. That alone might justify the certain long path of such a measure, which is sure to be opposed by some of the most expensive legal minds in the land.

In conjunction with the emergence of new leaders and a more amenable legal structure and to shorten the time frame in which real change can be brought about, we also desperately need enlightened institutional investors to step to the fore. They are, after all, the new majority owners of virtually all U.S. companies and many global ones as well, and they are uniquely suited to continue the fight where other forms of authority can't.

If and when new legislation of the type here proposed for Maine and elsewhere for the federal level begins to circumscribe corporate actions and if and when new leadership and their own excesses turn public opinion against them, corporations are certain to seek new domiciles abroad and in those lands with laws especially congenial to the retention of their power. (A corporation on the run looks surprisingly like a rogue financier on the run, for whom there is always a Cayman Island waiting.) Perhaps U.S. laws won't be able to reach the corporations in their new homes, but the large institutional investors can. They, too, are effectively borderless. Indeed, multinational institutional shareholding is virtually congruent with multinational corporations. By creating an enforceable code for owners and by insisting on adherence to it, the great funds can impose good governance notwithstanding the contrariety of most corporate laws or the distance the corporation manages to put between itself and the reach of U.S. law.

Let us fantasize one final time and imagine that these newly energized majority owners might create the kind of creative tension with management that could optimize both profits and the corporation's positive impact on society, including (as long as we're daydreaming) a voluntary agreement limiting corporate involvement in politics, elections, and referendum questions. Wouldn't that be wonderful? But institutional investors need not act out of such lofty, maybe even airy goals. Do it for cold-blooded bottom-line reasons—to eke out that extra 5 percent that the Corporate Library metric tells us is hidden by bad practices. But most of all, do it because it's the right thing. That's what is really needed over and above and along with everything else: a new culture of accountability.

Part of that is a fresh language that embraces economics but reflects the aspirations and needs of human beings far more fully than the language of modern economics alone ever can. Baseline words and phrases such as "profit" and "generally accepted accounting principles" have to be expanded holistically to include presently externalized or ignored costs. "Fiduciary" has to be rescued from the junk heap of empty words and restored to its etymological roots: the Latin *fiducia*, meaning "trust" and "confidence," akin to *fides*, as in "faith." Executives tell us they can manage only what they can measure. Fine, give them the tools to measure not just profit and loss but their impact on the larger society, and then give them a whole symphony of relevant languages—from environmental science to moral philosophy—to talk about what their new measures reveal.

The artifacts of accountability exist in great abundance. Legislative reform does not necessitate the Sisyphean prospect of going state to state and changing the laws one recalcitrant legislature at a time. Existing federal laws provide the core authority and framework for defining the responsibility of ownership. To be sure, the ancient rules of responsibility were specifically suspended with respect to investment in corporations under the doctrine of "limited liability"—a doctrine that might be the single most critical

factor accounting for the corporation's success as the premier wealth-creating mechanism in history. But ownership
responsibilities weren't suspended altogether. While individuals are legally entitled to ignore any incidents of ownership arising out of their stockholding in a company,
trustees serve as legal owners for the benefit of others and
must manage ownership responsibilities so as to maximize
the value of the trust estate.

If the meaning of fiduciary is today largely lost, an
echo of trusteeship and responsible ownership remains.
We have a collective memory of them. What we can
remember, we can enact and recreate. What's missing is
the culture to support and reinvigorate those artifacts—a
culture that would encourage banks, mutual funds, and
pension funds to rise above their own conflicts of interest—as well as embolden universities and foundations to
disturb existing profitable relationships in the name of
restoring accountability to our economic and financial
lives. That, I maintain, cannot be accomplished by legal
means alone. We need also to restore an ethical sense
for investors individually as owners and especially for
the large institutions that collectively hold the majority
position. That is where a culture of true accountability
must reside in the last analysis: on what is right as well as
on what is profitable. Doing good *and* doing well give
ethics the sinew and legs it needs.

The English scholars Anne Simpson, long the conscience of U.K. corporate governance, and the late
Jonathan Clarkham, with a distinguished career in the Bank
of England and as a member of the Cadbury Commission,
have suggested that corporate ownership of a significant
size—either as a percentage of the total or as a total value of
investment—imparts significant responsibilities that go well
beyond the normal bounds of economic language. In *Fair*

Shares: The Future of Shareholder Power and Responsibility, they write:

> The good working of the market-based system demands it for economic, social and political reasons. The economic reason is that there needs to be a mechanism for controlling boards that do not work well so as to prevent unnecessary waste of resources; the social reason is that listed companies are a crucial and integral part of the fabric of a modern society and their success reduces alienation; the political reason is that the limited liability company has achieved its far-sighted originators' aims beyond their wildest dreams, of producing concentrations of power and resources, and that those who exercise these powers must be effectively accountable for the way they do. The power and influence of the leaders of companies in domestic politics—and indeed internationally— are considerable.

I can't imagine the case being better put than that. The corporation is a creature of government. It was created by the political system. Thus, the language of politics ultimately must be resuscitated to restore *legitimacy* and *fiduciary* to their appropriate meanings in the modern world, and politics itself must be weaned from the corporate teat. Without that, everything else is wasted effort, but corporate hegemony won't be overthrown so easily. It depends on a culture that values and demands accountability. It requires courage in leadership. And it demands that those with a majority stake in the corpocracy—its principal owners and beneficiaries—lead the way back to the broad light of day. The hour is late. The sun won't always be waiting.

Appendix

The 10-year-old International Corporate Governance Network has developed a Statement of Principles on Institution Shareholder Responsibilities. The work was challenging in that the statement attempts to describe the entire gamut of rights and responsibilities of institutions, subject to the laws and customs of different cultures. Nonetheless, the document, as approved in January 2007, does an excellent job of laying out the obligation for trustees to use all incidents of ownership in a cost-effective manner so as to enhance the value of assets under management. I offer it here as a model of behavior for institutional investors generally.

The statement was developed by ICGN's Shareholder Responsibilities Committee, on which I serve. Other committee members include Peter Montagnon (Chair), Director of Investment Affairs, Association of British Insurers; Ramsay Brufer, Corporate Governance Manager, Alecta Pensionsforsakring, Omsesidigt; Stephen Davis, President, Davis Global Advisors; Yuji Kage, Managing Director, Pension Fund Association, Japan; Richard Koppes, of counsel, Jones Day; Michael McKersie, Manager, Investment Affairs,

Association of British Insurers; Colin Melvin, Chief Executive, Hermes Equity Ownership Services; Michael O'Sullivan, President, Australian Council of Superannuation Investors (ACSI); Christian Strenger, Company Director and Government Advisor, DWS Investment GmbH; and Anne Simpson (*ex officio*), Executive Director, International Corporate Governance Network.

Statement of Principles on Institutional Shareholder Responsibilities

Key Considerations

This ICGN statement sets out our view of the responsibilities of institutional shareholders, both in relation to their external role as owners of company equity and also in relation to their internal governance. Both are of concern to beneficiaries and other stakeholders. The ownership of equity carries important responsibilities, particularly due to voting rights that can influence the way in which a business is conducted. Ultimate owners cannot delegate these responsibilities. Even when they employ agents to act on their behalf, it is up to beneficial owners to ensure that those agents fulfill the responsibilities of ownership.

While some involved in the complex chain of intermediaries between beneficiaries and issuers have a simple obligation to provide a service, many have an agency function with a principal fiduciary responsibility to generate optimum returns consistent with the time horizon of the beneficiaries. Those who represent beneficiaries need to be clear about the objectives of the beneficiaries. This involves careful consideration of key points, including the appropriate balance between short-term return and long-term value. Resources applied to governance and the exercise of votes may generate costs in the short term, but an increasing weight of evidence suggests that this will add value in the long term. The ICGN Statement on Stock Lending explores aspects of this in greater detail.

While it is vital that companies ensure that shareholders can exercise their rights of ownership, these rights must be exercised responsibly. Moreover, responsible behavior on the part of shareholders will reinforce their claim to these rights. Even where companies refuse the rights of ownership to their shareholders, this does not absolve the latter from seeking to influence the behavior of the company. Responsible ownership requires high standards of transparency, probity, and care on the part of institutions, which may be met by adhering to the principles set out below. While practice varies in detail between national markets, the principles that underlie high standards are constant. The annex to this paper therefore includes examples of how principles have been applied in different markets to provide useful guidance. [The annex is available at the ICGN website, www.icgn.org. In addition, the ICGN website provides a bibliography of relevant literature.]This statement follows from the ICGN statement of October 2003. The principles listed here reflect the fact that understanding of the different roles played by principals and agents has developed substantially even in this relatively short time. Institutions that comply with the enlarged principles have a stronger claim both to the trust of their end beneficiaries and to the exercise of rights of equity ownership on their behalf.

Definitions

In this statement the terms "institution" and "institutional investor or shareholder" are used to refer to professional investors who act on behalf of beneficiaries, such as individual savers or pension fund members. Institutional shareholders may be the collective investment vehicles that pool the savings of many of the asset managers to whom they allocate the funds. Examples of the former include pension funds, insurance companies, and mutual funds. Investment arrangements for these institutional shareholders vary according to the types and local laws or regulations. What characterizes institutional investment is a separation of the ultimate beneficiary, for whom the investment is being made and who holds the economic interest, from the agent, who acts on behalf of the beneficiary.

The duty to act solely in the best interests of the beneficiary is called in some markets a "fiduciary" duty, which requires prudence, care, and loyalty. These duties cannot be delegated, even though the execution of the investment involves other parties, who are referred to as agents of the beneficiary. The beneficiary is also referred to as the *principal.* The agents in the process of investment have different roles and responsibilities. These agents form a chain of investment that can be complex depending on the particular arrangements made. Typically the chain includes:

A *governing body* responsible for overseeing the investment process and ensuring that other agents play their role in meeting the institution's objectives. The governing body may be a board of trustees, directors, or a sole individual, and beneficiaries may or may not have a role in their appointment, depending on the type of institution. The responsibilities of the governing body should be consistent with its objectives, and its operational and oversight role should be clearly defined. It should be clear to whom the governing body is accountable. The governing body is the first agent in the chain of investment.

Asset managers are the agents who are responsible for execution of the investment mandate set by the governing body. The asset manager may be employed directly by the governing body or be external and appointed on a contract. There may be a sole asset manager, or a series, for different asset categories or regions. The governance of the fund management body itself is also a relevant issue in considering the chain of investment. Fund managers may be publicly listed companies with shareholders and a board of directors. They may be privately owned or structured as a trust.

Service providers support the governing body in deciding on the fund manager's brief. For example, actuaries determine projected liabilities, and consultants may measure performance. Advisors may also be appointed by the governing body to assist with execution of the mandate—for example, through the appointment of research, advisory, or vote execution services, and in some cases, representation to companies on behalf of the governing body. While governing bodies may delegate certain functions to service providers, they should retain responsibility for the oversight and management of these providers.

Custodians are responsible for the safekeeping and maintenance of records for the assets of the fund, be these in electronic or paper form, including shares, cash deposits, and notary receipts. The custodian may subcontract part of this function—for example, to administrators of nominee accounts. Where this happens, institutions have a right to expect that subcustodians will recognize the natural rights of beneficial owners and their agents. Pension fund or other clients' assets should be legally separated from those of the custodian. The custodian cannot absolve itself of responsibility by entrusting to a third party all or some of the assets in its safekeeping. The ICGN Principles of Shareholder Responsibility are directed at all those in the investment chain who act as an agent for another party. This primarily means the first two parties in the investment chain as described above, namely the governing body and the asset managers. These in turn are responsible for securing the best quality contribution from service providers and custodians.

Internal Governance

As described above, different intermediaries in the institutional investment chain play different roles. Each intermediary should have internal governance arrangements that reflect the particular nature of their own role and responsibilities. The overarching obligation of each of the intermediaries is to safeguard the interests of beneficiaries. Four main elements apply to the internal governance of those involved in the investment chain if this fundamental principle is to be met:

1. *Oversight:* Arrangements for oversight of agents should be such that decisions taken at every stage along the investment chain reflect the interest of their ultimate beneficiaries. Governing bodies should have a structure and constitution that reflect this and which should be disclosed to beneficiaries. They should have mechanisms in place to receive feedback from beneficiaries and respond to their concerns.

   Governing bodies and, where relevant, individuals in a fiduciary position of responsibility for ultimate investors, such as pension fund trustees and representative boards, should be aware of their primary oversight role. They should be clear about the objectives of the beneficiaries, communicate them to portfolio managers and other agents employed, and ensure that they are being met. They should make clear which, if any, public or regulatory authorities have responsibility to monitor and enforce their fiduciary functioning. The way in which individuals are appointed to serve on the governing body should be disclosed as well as the criteria that are applied to such appointments. Such criteria should always take account of the need for expertise and understanding of the matters for which the governing body is responsible.

A most important factor is the behavior of those who sit on the governing body. It is essential that the oversight structure provides for robust decision making so that investment and voting decisions are taken in the interest of the beneficiaries and do not reflect other objectives of those involved. The structure of such bodies varies from market to market and may be determined by regulation or legislation. Whatever the structure, it is important that every individual who participates acts in an independent manner and in line with the overarching objective of safeguarding the best financial interests of beneficiaries. Such expectations should be set out clearly in the constitution of the governing body. Independent decision making is easier to achieve if the structure of the governing body is balanced with all relevant interests represented. In particular, it is not desirable that the plan sponsor or employer dominate the governing body. Where this is the case, consideration should be given to the representation of individuals accountable to beneficiaries even if this is not mandatory. A serious conflict of interest may also arise where the plan sponsor is a government or other public authority that may take voting and investment decisions that reflect their public policy objectives rather than the interests of the beneficiaries. Where this is the case, there is an additional need to ensure a majority of independent participants on the governing body.

2. *Transparency and accountability:* This requires regular disclosure to ultimate beneficiaries about material aspects of governance and organization. Governing bodies should develop clear standards with regard to governance of investee companies and links to the investment process through its impact on value, and for voting of shares and related issues, such as stock lending. The standards should inform their selection of portfolio managers and other agents. Governing bodies should be critical both in the selection of consultants and in evaluating the advice they receive from them, and ensure they receive value for the fees they pay, including for brokerage. Where they or their agents outsource services, they should disclose the name of the provider of the services in question, the nature of the mandate they have been given, and procedures for monitoring performance of the provider.

Governing bodies should hold their portfolio managers and other agents employed to account for adhering to the standards set for them. They should develop clear channels for communicating their policies to beneficiaries, their portfolio managers, and the companies in which they invest. They should regularly evaluate and communicate their achievements in meeting these policies. Asset managers and others in a similar agency position should also develop clear decision-making procedures and policies with regard to the governance of investee companies and for voting of shares held on behalf of clients. Their incentive structures should reflect the interests of the beneficiaries. Charges incurred on the behalf of clients, for example brokerage commissions and payment for research, should be justifiable. Asset managers should encourage brokers and research analysts whose services they use to factor governance considerations into their reports.

3. *Conflicts of interest:* Conflicts of interest inevitably arise from time to time. It is of paramount importance that these are recognized and addressed by governing bodies and other agents in the chain, if the overarching principle of safeguarding the interest of beneficiaries is to be respected. Those acting as agents should disclose all known potential conflicts of interest to their principal and explain how these are dealt with so as to protect their clients' interests. The governing body should have clear policies for managing conflicts and ensure that they are adhered to. This, in turn, requires an appropriate governance structure as set out above.

4. *Expertise:* Decision makers along all parts of the investment chain should be appropriately resourced and meet relevant standards of experience and skill in matters subject to deliberation. Governing bodies should have the right to outside advice, independent from any received by the sponsoring body. Portfolio managers and others in a similar agency position should deploy sufficient, qualified resources to meet clients' expectations. Delegation of key processes such as engagement with companies, voting decisions, and execution does not absolve agents involved in the investment process from their fiduciary responsibility to beneficiaries. They should be able to justify to beneficiaries specific actions taken on their behalf whether by themselves or by those to whom specific services are outsourced.

External Responsibilities

High standards of corporate governance make boards properly accountable to shareholders for the companies they manage on their behalf. They also help investee companies make sound decisions and manage risks to deliver sustainable and growing value over time. Pursuit of high standards of governance is therefore an integral part of institutions' fiduciary obligation to generate value for beneficiaries. It follows that corporate governance considerations should be integrated into the investment process. Moreover, general benefits from high standards of governance will accrue over time, only if all institutions are working to play an appropriate part.

Shareholder rights should always be exercised with the objective of delivering sustainable and growing value in mind. This requires attention to the specific situation of the company concerned, rather than the formulaic application of governance rules. Instead of seeking to interfere in the day-to-day management of the company, institutional shareholders and their agents should actively engage in a constructive relationship with investee companies to increase mutual understanding, resolve differences, and promote value creation. A relationship of trust is more likely to be achieved when institutional shareholders and their agents can demonstrate that they are exercising the rights of ownership responsibly. This includes:

Application of consistent policies: Just as it is important for beneficiaries to be informed of the governance policies adopted by those who act for them, so it is important for companies to be aware of the policies that shareholders are likely to adopt. In most markets, this has been made easier by the development of corporate governance codes that set standards for both sides to understand and apply. Shareholders should be clear about what standards they are applying and how they monitor investee companies. Where this could lead to a negative vote or an abstention at a general meeting, the company's board should be informed of this, ideally in writing, and of the reasons for the decision, at least in respect to significant holdings. Institutional shareholders should periodically measure and review the effectiveness of their monitoring and ownership activities and communicate the results to their beneficiaries, in such a way as to enhance their understanding without compromising specific engagement efforts.

Engagement with companies: Responsible owners should make use of their voting rights. A high voting turnout at general meetings helps ensure that decisions are sound and representative. Successful engagement, however, requires more than considered voting. It should also include: maintaining dialogue with the board on governance policies to address concerns before they become critical, supporting the company in respect of good governance, and consulting other investors and local investment associations where appropriate. When engaging with companies about governance issues, shareholders should respect market-abuse rules and not seek trading advantage through possession of price-sensitive information. Where appropriate and feasible, they may consider formally becoming insiders to support a process of longer-term change.

At the outset of engagement with companies, they should make it clear whether they wish to become insiders. They should encourage companies to ensure that all sensitive information and decisions resulting from engagement are made public for the benefit of all shareholders. They should consider working jointly with other shareholders on particular issues. In working with other investors, they should also respect rules with regard to concert parties. Institutions should encourage regulators to develop rules with regard to both market abuse and concertation that can be enforced sensibly and do not inhibit reasonable collaboration between shareholders or constructive dialogue more generally.

Investors should have a clear approach for dealing with situations where dialogue is failing. This should be communicated to companies as part of their corporate governance policy. Steps that may be taken under such an approach include: expressing concern to the board, either directly or in a shareholders' meeting; making a public statement; submitting resolutions to a shareholders' meeting; submitting one or more nominations for election to the board as appropriate; convening a shareholders' meeting; arbitration; and as a last resort, taking legal action, such as legal investigations or class actions.

Voting: Beneficial owners, or the governing bodies that invest on their behalf, have the ultimate right to vote. Markets collectively have a duty to oppose the abuse of voting power by those who do not enjoy beneficial ownership. Voting is not an end in itself but an essential means of ensuring that boards are accountable and fulfilling the stewardship obligation of institutions to promote the creation of value. Institutional shareholders should therefore seek to vote their shares in a considered way and in line with this objective. They should develop and publish a voting policy so that beneficiaries and investee companies understand what criteria are used to reach decisions. Voting decisions should reflect the specific circumstances of the case. Where this involves a deviation from the normal policy, institutions should be prepared to explain the reasons to their beneficiaries and to the companies concerned.

Asset managers should have appropriate arrangements for reporting to beneficiaries on the way in which voting policy has been implemented and on any relevant engagement with companies concerned. As a matter of best practice, they should disclose an annual summary of their voting records together with their full voting records in important cases. Voting records should include an indication of whether the votes were cast for or against the recommendations of the company management.

The ICGN encourages transparency, and consideration should be given to the merit of voluntary public disclosure of an asset manager's voting record as this may be of use in demonstrating a commitment to accountability and to show that conflicts of interest are being properly managed. As the level of public disclosure has increased in major markets, it is helpful if asset managers explain their thinking on public disclosure even when they have decided not to disclose. Institutions should seek to reach a clear decision either in favor or against each resolution. In defined or specific cases, institutions may wish to abstain to signal to the company either that it is in danger of losing support if it persists with a particular policy or that it is moving in the right direction but has not yet implemented an appropriate policy. In either case, the reason for the decision should be properly communicated to the company.

Where ownership responsibilities are outsourced, institutions should disclose the names of agents to whom they have outsourced together with a description of the nature and extent of this outsourcing and how it is regularly monitored. Where they feel it is not appropriate to name the agents they have employed, they should explain their reasons. Institutions should work proactively with other intermediaries and, where appropriate, regulators to remove barriers to voting wherever they occur in the chain.

Addressing corporate governance concerns: Institutions risk failing in their responsibilities as fiduciaries if they disregard serious corporate governance concerns that may affect the long-term value of their investment. They should follow up on these concerns and assume their responsibility to deal with them properly. Such concerns may relate to:

Transparency and performance, including the level and quality of transparency; the company's financial and operating performance, including significant strategic issues; substantial changes in the financial or control structure of the company; and the accounting and auditing practices of the investee company.

Board structures and procedures, including the role, independence, and suitability of nonexecutives and/or supervisory directors; the quality of succession practices and procedures; the remuneration policy of the company; conflicts of interest with large shareholders and other related parties; the composition and adequacy of the internal control systems and procedures; the composition of the audit and remuneration committees; and the management of environmental and ethical risks.

Shareholder rights, including the level and protection of shareholder rights; minority investor protection; proxy voting arrangements; and the independence of third-party fairness of opinions rendered on transactions.

Conclusion

Implementation of these principles by institutional share-holders will help generate sustainable returns for beneficiaries and secure a healthy corporate sector. The application of the principles set out here will vary according to market conditions, including the legal framework, but markets can learn from each other.

Notes

Chapter 1

"By December 2005, the *Economist* . . ." "Life after Lee," *Economist,* December 2005. www.economist.com/business /displaystory.cfm?story_id=E1_VPNSJPJ

"In 2003, according to . . ." "Executive Pay," *Forbes,* May 10, 2004. www.forbes.com/free_forbes/2004/0510/124.html

"I thought our comments . . ." *Wall Street Journal,* August 29, 2001.online.wsj.com/article/SB999035936679805198.html

Chapter 2

"The author James . . ." James Baldwin, "Stranger in the Village," in *In Depth: Essayists for Our Time,* 2nd ed. (Carl H. Klaus, Ed.)(San Diego, CA: Harcourt Brace Jovanovich, 1990), p. 72.

"There is no mention . . ." Peter Nobel, in a 2004 interview with Hazel Henderson for her syndicated column: "Abolish the 'Nobel' in Economics, Many Scientists Agree."

"As the late 19th-century . . ." Alfred Marshall, *Principles of Economics,* 8th ed. (London: Macmillan, 1920), I.I.1. Originally published in 1890.

"Economists have been acting . . ." *New York Times,* January 10, 2007.

"There is a larger issue . . ." David Gergen, *Harvard Gazette,* November 2–8, 2006, p. 13. HYPERLINK "http://www. nytimes.com/2007/01/10/business/10leonhardt.html?ei= 5070&en=0cb658252a7650ae&ex=1190260800&adxnnl=1 &adxnnlx =1190129387-XzTpjTwzoy9tkksHSPiL4A"

"As the *Economist* reported . . ." *Economist,* February 25, 2006 p. 28.

"Some scholars view . . ." Tamar Frankel in Peter Newman's, "Fiduciary Duties," in *The New Palgrave Dictionary of Economics and the Law,* vol. 2 (Peter Newman, ed) (New York: Palgrave Macmillan, 2004), p. 127.

Chapter 3

"Powell's nearly 40 . . ." A. C. Pritchard, "Justice Lewis F. Powell Jr. and the Counterrevolution in the Federal Securities Laws," 52 *Duke Law Journal,* 841,947.

"To give First Amendment . . ." Ted Nace, *Gangs of America: The Rise of Corporate Power and the Disabling of Democracy* (San Francisco: Berrett-Koehler, 2003, 2005), p. 169.

Chapter 4

"By the mid-1990s . . ." John C. Coffee Jr., *Gatekeepers: The Role of the Professions in Corporate Governance* (Oxford, England: Oxford University Press, 2006).

Chapter 5

"Through his book . . ." Bill George, *Authentic Leadership: Secrets to Creating Lasting Value* (San Francisco: Jossey-Bass, 2004).

Chapter 6

"As one of the . . ." My classroom notes from 1957.

"Stockbrokers watched each other . . ." Robert J. Cole, *New York Times,* May 2, 1975. select.nytimes.com/gst/abstract.html? F40D15F63D5F14738DDDAB0894DD405B858BF1D3

"Not only did the numbers . . ." Derek Bok, *The Cost of Talent* (New York: Free Press, 1993), p. 89.

"The only perfomance that counts . . ." Peter Drucker, "Corporate Takeovers: What Is to Be Done?" *Public Interest,* Winter 1986, pp. 3–24.

Chapter 7

"You know what the . . ." *New York Times,* April 21, 2006. select.nytimes.com/search/restricted/article?res=FA0D 15FF3E5B0C728EDDAD0894DE404482

"What used to be conflict . . ." *Money,* April 25, 2002. money.cnn.com/2002/04/25/pf/investing/money_ grubman/index.htm

"Hidden portfolio transaction . . ." John C. Bogle, *The Battle for the Soul of Capitalism* (New Haven, CT: Yale University Press, 2005).

"The idea is an old one . . ." Michael Jensen, *Harvard Business Review,* September/October 1989. harvardbusi nessonline.hbsp.harvard.edu/b02/en/common/item_ detail.jhtml?id=89504&referral=2342

"If you examine all the . . ." Henry Kravis, Keynote Speech delivered at Dow Jones Private Equity Conference, New York City, September 22, 2004.

Chapter 9

"According to Knut Kjaer . . ." *Guardian,* May 22, 2006. business.guardian.co.uk/story/0,,1780129,00.html

"While it is naïve to . . ." *Lancet,* vol. 369, no. 9557 (2007), p. 163

" While shareholder activism . . ." Patty Stonesifer, Letter to the Editor, *Los Angeles Times,* January 14, 2007, p.M5

"Ownership fragmented into shares . . ." Abram Chayes in the Introduction to John P. Davis's, *Corporations: A Study of the Origin and Development of Great Business Combinations and of their Relation to the Authority of the State,* 2nd ed. (New

York: Capricorn Books, 1961), p. xviii. Originally published in 1904.

"We may grant . . ." Adolph Berle and Gardiner Means, *The Modern Corporation and Private Property,* rev. ed. (New York: Harcourt Brace & World, 1967), p. 311.

"Few directors in modern times . . ." Federal Reserve Chairman Alan Greenspan addressed the topic of corporate governance at the Stern School of Business at New York University on March 26, 2002.

Chapter 10

"Ralph Nader struck back . . ." *Unsafe at Any Speed,* exp. ed. (New York: Bantam, 1973); *Taming the Giant Corporation* (New York: Norton, 1976).

"The rationale for democracy . . ." Charles E. Lindbloom, *The Market System* (New Haven, CT: Yale University Press, 2001), p. 239.

"The good working of the . . ." Anne Simpson and Jonathan Clarkham, *Fair Shares: The Future of Shareholder Power and Responsibility* (Oxford, England: Oxford University Press, 1999). p. 224.

Index